AQUATIC CENTER MARKETING

Judith Leblein Josephs

HUMAN KINETICS

Library of Congress Cataloging-in-Publication Data

Names: Josephs, Judith Leblein, 1955- author.
Title: Aquatic center marketing / Judith Leblein Josephs.
Description: Champaign, IL : Human Kinetics, [2019] | Includes bibliographical references.
Identifiers: LCCN 2018019648 (print) | LCCN 2018035440 (ebook) | ISBN 9781492572800 (ebook) | ISBN 9781492526261 | ISBN 9781492526261q(print)
Subjects: LCSH: Aquatic sports--Marketing. | Amusement parks--Marketing. | Recreation centers--Marketing.
Classification: LCC GV191.67.W3 (ebook) | LCC GV191.67.W3 J67 2019 (print) | DDC 797--dc23
LC record available at https://lccn.loc.gov/2018019648

ISBN: 978-1-4925-2626-1 (print)

The web addresses cited in this text were current as of July 2018, unless otherwise noted.

Senior Acquisitions Editor: Michelle Maloney; **Acquisitions Editor:** Tom Heine; **Developmental Editor:** Anne Hall; **Managing Editor:** Ann C. Gindes; **Copyeditor:** Alisha Jeddiloh; **Permissions Manager:** Martha Gullo; **Graphic Designer:** Whitney Milburn; **Cover Designer:** Keri Evans; **Cover Design Associate:** Susan Rothermel Allen; **Photographs (cover and interior):** © Judith Leblein Josephs unless otherwise noted; **Photo Production Manager:** Jason Allen; **Printer:** Versa Press

Human Kinetics books are available at special discounts for bulk purchase. Special editions or book excerpts can also be created to specification. For details, contact the Special Sales Manager at Human Kinetics.

Printed in the United States of America 10 9 8 7 6 5 4 3 2 1

The paper in this book is certified under a sustainable forestry program.

Human Kinetics
P.O. Box 5076
Champaign, IL 61825-5076
Website: www.HumanKinetics.com

In the United States, email info@hkusa.com or call 800-747-4457.
In Canada, email info@hkcanada.com.
In the United Kingdom/Europe, email hk@hkeurope.com.

For information about Human Kinetics' coverage in other areas of the world, please visit our website: **www.HumanKinetics.com**

E6743

This book is dedicated to my mom and dad, Ida and Fred Leblein, who understood the value of having their city kids learn to swim. My early swimming experiences at Boylan Street Pool in Newark, New Jersey, which cost only 10 cents a swim, have resulted in a lifetime commitment to aquatic management.

CONTENTS

ACKNOWLEDGMENTS

I thank all the staff members and elected officials throughout my career who have tolerated my unique and unusual approaches to marketing, with special thanks to the past and present staff of the Summit Family Aquatic Center and the City of Summit's Department of Community Programs. Their creative and tireless efforts on behalf of the residents of Summit are stellar. Thank you, Jamie Colucci, for assisting me with the photography in the book and for your constant encouragement. I am indebted to Sophie Mannaerts, David Guida, and Gretchen Masterfano for their acceptance of my never-ending desire to dazzle our residents.

Thank you to those brave city managers whom I challenged, infuriated, and entertained over my 30 years in public life, especially Lane Biviano, Greg Fehrenbach, Jack Coughlin, Chris Cotter, and Michael Rogers. It was my mission to make them laugh whenever possible, and they significantly influenced my career.

I admire and thank Lou Mason Neely, finance officer with the Township of East Brunswick, who was a mentor, friend, and spiritual advisor throughout the creation and success of Crystal Springs Family Aquatic Center. When the going got tough, Lou was always there.

I have overwhelming gratitude to Chuck Neuman of Water Technology, who saw talent in me and encouraged my professional development on an international level. For that I will always be grateful. A special shout out to Josh Brenner, who met me when I was a young, enthusiastic recreation director and gave me a chance at a great opportunity for professional development.

My family deserves all the credit for sticking with me throughout this book process and never letting me quit! To the long suffering Jim Josephs, thank you for listening to me complain about the book and then celebrating with me the minute it was finished. And I'm sorry to my siblings and family members who often made excuses for my absence at family events as I traveled the world assisting clients.

To the clients of Water Technology and JLJ Enterprises who are mentioned in this book, I thank you for welcoming me to your team and letting me play a small role in your success.

INTRODUCTION

If you have ever wished you had more money to spend on marketing, or better yet, wished you had a staff for marketing and promotion, this book is for you. The operation of a successful aquatic center takes a talented staff with safety and operations as their primary concern. But as competition for the leisure dollar increases with changing trends in how people spend their leisure time, aquatic facilities are now challenged to be competitive in both marketing and promotions. Owners and managers of facilities must respond with effective promotions and communication with their membership.

Written with the aquatic professional in mind, *Aquatic Center Marketing* introduces practical, affordable, and innovative marketing concepts that will be helpful to new and aging aquatic facilities of all sizes. Whether you are working with a public, private, or commercial property, these tried-and-tested techniques can increase your attendance and revenue, reenergize your staff, and establish your value in the community.

If you have felt the increasing pressure of creating and sustaining revenue-positive aquatic functions, you have to take a comprehensive look at your branding and marketing campaigns. Not formally trained in marketing and communications? No problem! This guide can help you achieve success with a step-by-step approach to building your brand or reigniting your image.

Aquatic managers faced with aging facilities must learn to pump up the volume on their marketing to increase the perceived value of their product and ensure public support for building new facilities or renovating existing ones. It's no longer enough to justify aquatic operations with the value of aquatics as a lifetime activity. Although swimming remains a popular recreation activity in the United States, its ranking continues to fall as new trends in fitness, exercise, and sport climb in popularity. It's no longer enough to just offer recreational and competitive aquatics; it's now vital to create an experience. An entire generation of families has come to expect more exciting and interactive pools from the smallest roadside motel to the latest water-park hotels. Private swim clubs, YMCAs, fitness centers, swim schools, and competitive venues are all competing for customers seeking not only swimmable water but aquatic entertainment—or aqua-tainment, as I like to call it.

Whether you are responsible for a public swim facility, aquatic club, small to midsized waterpark, resort, or lakefront venue, you will face increasingly higher expectations for cost recovery and revenue enhancements while managing shrinking advertising and promotional budgets. There are hundreds of thousands of commercial pools in the United States alone. Are you ready to go head to head with all of this competition for the aquatic dollar?

Like many other people responsible for promoting an aquatic facility, I haven't had extensive formal training in marketing and public relations, but I have always been a great observer of the human experience. As a child, I was always curious as to why people behave the way they do. What is their motivation to choose one activity over another? What makes them happy? What makes them buy one item over another? I challenge you to become a great observer of your guests' behaviors. Reach outside the aquatic management world and become an observer of advertising, television, and marketing concepts used in other industries. With the help of the concepts shared in this book, you will be able to apply your observations to actions that will make your facility a success.

So how does a kid from a housing project in Newark, New Jersey, find her way to a career in aquatics? It all started with a magical experience on a hot asphalt playground. My sisters and I would pack a little picnic of saltine crackers and bring our blanket along on summer days. Our trip was only yards away from our three-bedroom apartment, but that trip brought us to a place that seemed like a beach resort. A large galvanized pole reaching out of the ground beckoned children from the neighborhood to dance and play under a cool spray that erupted from the cap on top of the pole. We never quite knew where or how the water got there; we were just delighted to share it with our friends. As we got older, we did come to realize that the maintenance man with a big key would disappear underground and turn on the pump. The showers, as we called them, would come on first as a dribble and then as a rising cloud of relief. We were teased when they would first shut off, and we would rise up and chant "We want more!" until we got an encore spray. When our chanting didn't work anymore, there was a collective sigh and we would all grab our blankets and retreat home, exhausted from a day of play under the showers. Some 50 years later, the concept now thrives in water-play areas around the world—at a much higher cost, I must say, but the equation remains true: Children plus water equals fun!

When I was old enough to march behind my sister to Boylan Street Pool, the magic of the showers was diminished by a beautiful blue pool. We went there daily for 10 cents a swim, and the experience changed my life. One day I took notice of a beautiful woman gliding effortlessly through the water with hardly a ripple left behind. From that moment on I wanted to be her. My love affair with aquatics began with learn-to-swim classes and then on to swim team; the summers couldn't be long enough. On our walks home we'd get a lemon ice and maybe stop at the penny candy store. That was living for a kid from the projects.

The true inspiration for a lifetime of promoting all things aquatic came when my mom, a fan of old movies, shared a film featuring Esther Williams as the million-dollar mermaid. An angel who could swim underwater while smiling and dive from a tower as gracefully as a bird was now my muse. I watched those old musicals with my mom and wanted to be just like Williams.

These experiences taught me the impact that aquatics could have on a child's life. From the showers to Boylan Street to a career traveling around the world talking about aquatics, it became clear to me that the visual images, the emotions, and the entire aquatic environment made memories and changed lives. It was not only the human desire to be around water; it was the total experience.

I've come to understand and can now share within the pages of this book how to become a trend watcher. In the delivery of exceptional aquatic programs, everything and everyone matters. From signage, brand development, and social networking to mascots, promotional events, and membership premiums, this book will cover it all.

The book begins with part I on brand management. In these two chapters you'll learn how to create a brand identity for your facility or refresh a brand that no longer works for you or has grown stale. Even the most successful international corporations revisit their brands regularly and find new ways of delivering their message. You should too.

In part II, the next four chapters cover effective ways to build community support for building a new facility or adding a new attraction. Aquatic centers can only thrive within a community that understands the economic value they bring to the area. This understanding is essential to securing local funding or project approval through the zoning and planning approval phases. The chapters in this part also discuss ways to excite guests, appeal to specific populations, and use smart pricing.

Part III is all about internal and external communication. With so many information outlets now available, the challenge is getting noticed, developing a following, and keeping followers' attention. This is especially challenging during difficult times or when a facility must recover from an incident. Social media and the digital age of communication require fast responses to these demands. You need every possible communication tool ready to meet these challenges.

Facilities with limited marketing resources will love part IV. These two chapters explore not only explore how to increase your bottom line but also how to get others to do it for you. The Tom Sawyer School of

Marketing is my concept based on the classic theme of making it look like fun so others will do your work. Intriguing, eh?

As you race through the chapters of this book, you'll come to see that it is not about how much you spend on marketing but how effective your efforts are. An effective marketing plan is much like baking a delicious cake. If you have all the right ingredients in place, layer by layer, you will ultimately end up with a tasty and satisfying treat!

PART I

BRAND MANAGEMENT

1

DEVELOP A BRAND IDENTITY

As a child of the 1950s, my first exposure to the word *brand* was from the many Western TV shows I watched on Saturday mornings while eating my cereal. Cattle were wrangled into a corral and then branded with a hot iron. This brand could then be used to identify the steer's owner in case of loss or theft. Some brands included unique letters, scripts, and symbols that could also be seen on iron gates leading to the ranch house. The rancher's reputation was carried by his brand. Were his cattle well fed? Would they sell at a high price? Was the rancher an honest man? Ranchers took pride in the look of the brand each steer carried, and they would boast of their brand at the end of the day, with one foot up on a brass bar rail.

Today, the word *brand* is bandied about in all kinds of ways, from *personal brand* to *internal branding* to *brand management and development* to *brand identity*. But, if you were to ask people what the definition of *brand* is, you would get a myriad of answers. Some think their logo is their brand, while others think it is a combination of logo, reputation, vision, organization, and service.

The American Marketing Association (AMA) defines *brand* as "a name, term, design, symbol or any other feature that identifies one seller's good or service as distinct from those of other sellers. The legal term for brand is trademark. A brand may identify one item, a family of items, or all items of that seller. If used for a firm as a whole, the preferred term is trade name" (American Marketing Association n.d.).

Merriam-Webster defines *brand* as "a category of products that are all made by a particular company and all have a particular name" and "a particular kind or type of something." That may seem confusing. But *Merriam-Webster* also provides another definition, "to put a mark on to show ownership," and some synonyms: "engrave, etch, impress, imprint, infix, ingrain, also engrain." Now we're getting somewhere! The synonyms paint a much clearer picture of all the things a good brand can accomplish.

What Is Your Brand?

Your brand is made up of so many things. It is your facility's identity. It's what your facility represents, including your vision, your story, and your role in the community. It should be an image that translates to the experience, impression, and service you provide your members.

Your brand is then communicated through your signage, logo, public relations, programs, activities, social media, colors, mascots, and customer experience. You build your brand with layers that are carefully planned and can grow with the brand. Some brands become timeless, while others grow old. Even top international companies revisit their brands to make sure they reflect the current vision of the company and its products.

When done well, your brand can increase the perceived value of your organization by making it stand out among others. The stronger the brand, the stronger the perceived value of your facility will be. It all adds up to a healthy financial picture, community support for future projects, and a sense of ownership from customers and clients. In the battle to capture the leisure dollar, the choices are ever expanding, from trampoline and zip-line parks to themed restaurant arcades, and an aquatic venue must have a brand that establishes it as the top choice.

A good brand can deliver your message. It's a way to connect with potential customers and motivate them to return, bringing other new customers with them. Creating a strong brand is also important because the general public, fueled by social media, is quick to brand a facility. Wouldn't you rather control the creation of your brand before they do?

How do you brand for success? The creation of a logo and a tagline is not the end of the brand journey, but it's a good place to start. Once you've created your brand, you have to keep your message consistent and deliver a great customer experience time after time. You must keep your promises to your members and continually earn and keep their trust. This commitment extends to your corporate partners, benefactors, employees, and advertisers as well. It's all wrapped up in the brand like a package tied with a bow.

JUDITH'S GEMS

I worked on developing the sign plan for the Chandler Park Family Aquatic Center with the staff of Wayne County Parks in Michigan. Chandler Park was already a park in Detroit, but the new family aquatic center was to be the only wave pool in the city. It was obvious that a wave over the city would be an outstanding logo, and thus the brand was born. The corner of each sign throughout the site includes a simple wave that mirrors the park logo. The mascots include Wayne, Wanda, and Willy, a family of whales that is found throughout the facility and featured on the signage in various forms of attire.

Logo

Let's start with the logo. You want your logo to be the symbol that best represents your aquatic center. You want it to be as timeless, or evergreen, as possible. A successful logo can be identified even without words or a tagline. Colors and graphics are vital to helping people easily recognize your logo and understand your story. The wordmark, or logotype, is crucial as well. Can it stand alone, like Coca-Cola or Nike? Is it playful? Is it serious? Is it timely? Be careful to make your logo separate from your wordmark. With time and hard work, both should be easily recognized. Remember that the logo needs to be readily identified and will translate to your signage, letterhead, website, uniforms, and press materials. Consistently placing your logo throughout your facility and within print and electronic media is paramount to your success.

Pick your colors well when branding your aquatic center. Again, the colors in your logo should carry a message that is timeless. Beware of colors that are trendy; they will quickly age. I often equate color selection to buying a house. If you look at a house that has green or brown shag carpeting, you know that house hasn't had work done since the 1970s. Bright, trendy colors like fuchsia also age your message the way a tie-dyed T-shirt ages your wardrobe. In addition, color schemes are vital to delivering your brand message, but they can be a maintenance nightmare when matching marketing pieces and signage to your logo. Colors with red pigment don't hold up well in the aquatic environment and tend to fade. Years down the road, you may regret your color choices.

Matching your colors to your theme can get tricky. If you are going for a woodland theme, then using tropical colors is a mistake. If your facility is geared toward young families, then primary colors make perfect sense. Become a student of the psychology of color. For instance, yellow and red promote excitement and entice the appetite. Those colors are known to excite children.

Color selection can also affect your bottom line. Early meetings with your sign manufacturer and printer to determine what colors are stock items and what colors are special orders can help keep your budget manageable. Sometimes, just one step lower on the PMS (Pantone Matching System) chart of colors can save thousands in the promotion of your brand.

If you have the budget to work with an experienced logo designer, be sure to share your vision and message well. Be prepared to share your concepts, design documents, and theming with the artist. Some of the best logos I've worked on have come from young artists working at local sign shops. They are talented, hungry for experience, and affordable. If their age matches your target market, it's even better. They'll know how to translate your message through images.

Whether you do some of the work yourself or work with an agency, you still should be the driving force in the brand creation. Make sure the logo will translate well on paper, electronic media, hats, T-shirts, and promotional items. Complicated, four-color logos may be appealing but will cost more in setup charges as you develop promotional pieces, uniforms, and signage. For those with a small budget, be sure the logo is effective in black and white. Simple, easily identified, and timeless logos are the most successful. Online design services are available at discounted prices, and those who are on a truly tight budget and are tech savvy may find this type of service is their answer. I've found there is nothing like the personal touch when trying to convey emotions, feelings, and passion, all necessary components in the development of a logo.

Beware of logo design contests. Public entities are notorious for proposing contests that result in designs that are not well thought out for the facility mission and goals. If forced into this type of promotional activity, reserve the right to refuse or use parts of the design. You have to live with that logo for years; the amateur artist spends the prize money and moves on.

I'm not totally against gathering ideas through social media or focus groups; I've seen them work in creating buzz about a new facility. But in my experience, having an eight-year-old brand an aquatic facility just doesn't work. That doesn't mean you shouldn't listen and be open to a kid's ideas, however. Gather a group of your target-market youth and have some fun with them, but don't promise to use their ideas. Sometimes, you will find a pearl of wisdom that can work for you.

Branding Challenges

My first experience branding a new facility was a challenging one that has stood the test of time. The Township of East Brunswick in central New Jersey operated a small swimming lake with brackish water that was nestled in a beautiful wooded area. Dallenbach Lake, operated by the Department of Recreation, had been a favorite swimming facility of the community for generations. Changing attitudes toward lake swimming, new environmental concerns about freshwater treatment, and a shrinking membership all contributed to a master plan and controversial proposal to replace the old swimming hole with a state-of-the-art family aquatic center. The lake, although maintained as a healthy swimming environment, felt dark and dirty to many new residents who grew up swimming in pools. An occasional encounter with a snake or other wildlife didn't help. But there was a romantic sense of nostalgia that made the public outreach and consensus-building campaign difficult. Although many residents who opposed the project had not been guests for years, they held childhood memories that prevented them from envisioning the future of the facility. After years of hard work, the project became a reality, and it still operates today as a financial asset to the township and an exceptional aquatic experience for its members.

My challenge with this project was creating a new brand that was exciting and totally different from the Dallenbach Lake brand. From the naming of the facility to its tagline, color scheme, and logo, the vision was that of a bright, clean, and sparkling experience. Once we focused on the vision and the perception we hoped to create, the rest was easy. Working with a local sign manufacturer, the Crystal Springs Family Aquatic Center brand was born. Years later, it was rebranded as Crystal Springs Family Waterpark after the fear of using the term waterpark had passed with the facility's years of success.

The name Crystal Springs came from the concept that the old swimming facility was spring fed and the new one is crystal clear. From that name arose the tagline, The Gem of the Park System. Nothing shines more than diamonds, and thus the logo was born. The diamond theme, although not obviously aquatic, still delivered the message that the facility was sparkling clean. The logo and sign plan carried the symbol and colors of the diamond centerpiece throughout the facility. The signs, crafted from carved wood, were coated with glass silica so the logo would shine in the sun. On opening day, community leaders and local dignitaries received a small jewelry box with a crystal inside. These crystals, purchased at a local craft shop, made a huge impression. T-shirts in the gift shop were themed with diamonds, and crystals were sold along with other shiny promotional items. Crystals were attractive, readily available, and relatable to the guests. The campaign was timeless and continues to be used today. When your logo, tagline, and mascot can be easily printed or purchased without needing customization, your revenue on merchandise per guest, or per cap, will grow your bottom line.

There is a caveat to creating a brand that focuses on cleanliness. You must always maintain that promise. If the facility were allowed to show its age, have unclean restrooms, or look dingy, the promise made by the brand would be tarnished. You must stand behind your brand and continually renew the message. Otherwise, the new negative brand

What started as Crystal Springs Family Aquatic Center in 1994 was later renamed to Crystal Springs Family Waterpark when it expanded years later.

created on social media will far outweigh the original intention when the brand was developed. Years ago, those in the industry would say that one unhappy visitor will tell eight others, those eight will tell eight more, and so on. Today, with social media your facility can become a worldwide Instagram sensation, with thousands having an opinion.

I spent 10 years working with an international aquatic design firm as an operations analyst. My job was to assist communities with their new aquatic centers, and I had some amazing experiences while helping communities with branding. For many municipal agencies, branding was a foreign experience. For example, Glen Rock, New Jersey, was committed to a new facility but was not ready to offer a carnival-type experience. Known as an upscale community with an understated elegance, creating a brand posed a huge challenge. Where others were open to primary colors and striped umbrellas, they would have none of that. What resulted was a theme that matched their sensibilities at that time. Flowers adorned each area, white picket fencing separated the children's pool from the main pool, and plaid umbrellas were special ordered to complete the yuppie experience of the 1990s. This approach was different but appropriate in matching the community brand. The creativity of the atmosphere made up for the fact that the recreation department was forced to use the city logo, with no reference to swimming or aquatics—another lesson in making the brand match the community.

In Indiana, I worked on another unique project that was an outstanding example of matching the community brand with the branding for a new aquatic venue. A bit of history helps explain the challenge: Governor of Indiana and later U.S. president William Henry Harrison was a member of the Whig Party. A popular campaign song for the Whig Party was credited with Harrison's win over incumbent president Martin Van Buren. The song and campaign slogan of "Tippecanoe and Tyler Too" became an important part of Indiana history. So, when creating a new aquatic center for Lafayette, Indiana, the staff and I were charged with creating a branding strategy using the name Tropicanoe Cove and a tropical theme.

The merging of the Tippecanoe legend and the word *tropical* set the tone for an unusual branding challenge. With a unique name, the only answer was to focus on tropical colors and nautical theming. This was done in every part of the park, even in painting some of the pipes and mechanical areas that were visible to the guests. The branding focus was on fun, color, and island fun since the name of the brand itself wasn't an easy sell. Tropicanoe Cove has kept its promises to its guests for years and has branded itself as the fun place to be in Lafayette.

Revamping Your Brand

One of the most popular segments on television shows today is the makeover. From finding a new wardrobe, haircut, or clothing style to finding a new love, people binge-watch others reinventing themselves. Reinventing your facility or revamping your brand isn't as simple as a new coat of paint. Just like developing a brand for a new facility, reinventing a brand is a multilayered approach that takes thought, stakeholder input, and imagination. Facilities that seek to redefine what they stand for in the minds of prospective customers and current members must take an honest look at how they are currently perceived and identify what they would like to be known for in the future. This is an easier process when you are rehabilitating an aging facility and offering an exciting new aquatic center. It's a much more difficult task when rebuilding a reputation after a tragedy or poor performance.

Can You Handle the Truth?

The first step in revamping your brand is to find out how you are currently perceived in the community. Your brand is not what you hope it to be; it is what the community thinks of you now. Are you known as the old, tired aquatic center? Are stories of poor management or bad maintenance permeating social media? Is your management team seen as unresponsive and lazy? These things may not be true, but public perception is everything, especially in these times of social media, Yelp, and other visitor comment sites. There may be a huge difference between how others see you and how you see yourself.

Interviews, focus groups, and online surveys will shed some light on public perception of your aquatic center and on the strengths and weaknesses of your operation and staff. You have to be willing to listen to customers, including those who no longer come to the facility. You can gain great insight from both current members and those who have moved on. There's a tendency in park and recreation organizations to preach to the congregation. Yes, it's important to know what current members think and need, but what about those who left? Why did they leave? Was it price? Was it reputation? Were these claims valid? If we don't ask, we will never know. Most of us in this business are people pleasers or folks with a sense of service in our hearts. We have a tendency to answer a complaint quickly, without fully listening or identifying the real basis for the complaint. During this phase of revamping your brand, talk less and listen more!

The suggestions offered on brand identity can't substitute for revamping your brand. You can pour all of your funding and energy into those things, but in revamping your brand you have to truly reinvent yourself and show substantive improvement in your efforts and mission. A facility must improve its service, take a different approach to customers, and work hard to make drastic changes and react to those items that rise to the top in the discovery phase of revamping the brand.

Branding often involves lots of words and photos. But revamping your brand takes meaningful action and a focus on providing members with a total experience. Aquatic facilities are not just for swimming anymore; they should be the center of community life. They need a visible change in actions, not just in image, and this change has to be consistent, reliable, and relatable.

Brand reinvention can be simultaneous with creating a new facility or undertaking a major renovation. In fact, rebranding in those situations is much easier than recovering from a tragedy or poor public image. Sometimes, revamping a brand comes with new leadership in the organization, a new form of management, or a new direction driven by decreasing revenue. When revamping your brand, tell the story of why the change is coming. Provide the reason for the new look. This story has to be accepted and believed by you and your staff. When staff members embrace the change, others will follow, so they are key to the success of this conversion. They are just as important in delivering the message as all the promotional items you are sure to incorporate. You will have to convince everyone involved that this is a new facility with a new look. Let everyone know how special the aquatic center is. Treat your facility in that way and others will follow suit.

Honest reinvention is not easy, but it is often necessary. Even the largest, most successful companies do some level of brand reinvention. Aquatic professionals should be reinventing themselves and their facilities in some aspect every several years. A complete revamping of your brand will start the process and will require hard work. Retooling and updating will be much easier and more affordable. Existing brands have numerous advantages over new brands: They can lean on their name recognition, their current customer base, and their revenue.

Who Are You, and How Did You Come to Be?

Understanding the history and evolution of your aquatic center is a great start. Before you can reinvent the facility, you have to know why it was built, along with the original mission and vision. Sometimes the mission changes with each new director or change in the political body. Getting back to the reason the facility was built may even help you to design the new brand. Look at the history with fresh eyes, take from it what you can, and bring it into present thinking to create your new approach. How has the industry changed? Have you moved away from the initial role or purpose of the facility? Pay homage to the past with a modern twist, and you could avoid upsetting those in the community who continue to support the facility and embrace its history. Answer some of these questions and you are on your way.

Honor Your Client Base

Remember that you already have a base membership that still believes in your facility. Honor and engage those members. Change to a brand can be controversial because people in general don't welcome change. Public entities find it difficult to accept change, and they approach it with trepidation. As you create your new brand, match your new programs and activities to the new brand while keeping in mind your membership base. They have been loyal and need to feel valued as you embark on your new brand.

Reach the Super Influencers

It's important to share your new brand with those who write local travel blogs, participate in elite swim groups, and are well-known community members who use social media. They are the super influencers or key communicators in the community—win them over, and they will bring along the others. Refer to the facility's new name in every conversation, in every article, and at every opportunity. Where others still refer to *the pool* when its new name is *family aquatic center*, repeat the name over and over until you can't falter and it catches on. From answering the phone to giving presentations in the community, repeat the name as often as you can stand it! Revamped brands must restore their bond with their members. The age of social media challenges the marketers of aquatic centers to become more creative and adaptable to the realities of communication today.

Every Change May Not Stick

Revamping your brand can certainly result in improved memberships, clients, and daily visitors, but not every idea will be a winner. Don't let that discourage you. Stick to the new programs and concepts as part of your revamping and know that the strongest will survive; however, you must carefully analyze each new change and be patient. Sometimes revamping the brand of an aquatic center takes an entire generation. Your loyal members may never use the new name or tagline when referring to your facility and may in fact resent it. But, be patient! With time, the next generation will only know the new brand.

Social Consciousness and Charitable Marketing

Just as styles change, so do marketing campaigns and priorities. Revamping your brand is an opportunity to embrace new efforts in the world of marketing and make social consciousness and charitable marketing components of your new brand. Yes, major companies and government-run facilities have always provided social services and scholarships as part of their standard operating procedures, but they didn't tell anyone. It was a well-kept secret unless you were a beneficiary. This type of charity through business makes an impact on today's consumer, and it is one of the reasons a consumer remains loyal to a brand.

Focus on programming that helps others. Food drives, scholarship fund-raisers, Swim-a-Thons, and the promotion of these concepts at the center of your brand will differentiate you from others. If you incorporate conservation and energy savings into your new brand, you will also capture the attention of potential customers who are influenced by this focus. If you have any doubts about how charitable commerce works, just research the shoe company TOMS or the sock company Bombas.

Prove Your Value to the Community

At every opportunity, share your new brand and your mission with the public in every form possible. Use every facet of social media to let the community know your new brand and share your vision. Blogs, videocasts, podcasts, and radio and television spots highlighting your changes are essential. In doing so, you can become more than just an aquatic center and share the positive impact you have on the local economy. Do people purchase bathing suits and towels to visit your facility? Do they stop to buy gasoline when they visit your water park? Are they purchasing food to bring along for a picnic? How many young people do you hire and provide with skills training? Do you offer safety education that has saved lives in the community? Once you establish your brand, reinforce it by becoming the local authority on water safety, whether your guests are with you or somewhere else. Teaching them how to save themselves and others is a valuable tool in your reinvention. It is vital to share your positive financial and safety impact on the community with those who are in a position to support you.

From Summit Board of Recreation to Summit Community Programs—The Birth of a Brand

I've been involved in branding many new and improved aquatic centers in my role as an aquatic operations analyst, but the Summit Community Programs opportunity was a real challenge. It included the rebranding of an entire recreation department, community pools, and municipal golf course. I became the director of a newly formed Department of Community Programs that had been a Board of Recreation for over 50 years. A series of task-force meetings had resulted in the creation of this new department with the following goals.

1. To create a new department combining current programs and enhancing youth services, senior services, and recreation
2. To rethink and restate an overall mission and to create a new board to fulfill the mission and an organizational structure to optimize service delivery for all constituents

They established the following:

Mission—To provide recreational and other related programs and services that meet the community's needs, with a special consideration for seniors and youth

Values—Affordability, character development, communication, excellence, friendliness, health and wellness, inclusiveness, learning, partnerships, and responsiveness

Vision—To serve as the community's prime source for recreation for both youth and seniors, providing excellent programs, facilities, services, and information

This was a textbook start to the rebranding of this new department and a great example of the focus-group and task-force work that should begin the process. So now the new department had a name: the Department of Community Programs. But the city still needed to create a brand that would replace the name of the former department, pay homage to the legacy of the former organization, and create a sense of excitement about the new direction of this expanded department.

As the director of this new initiative, I was charged with developing the new brand with little to no budget. Ten years later, the layers we created added up to a brand that is now easily recognizable, has the confidence of the community, and has become identified not only by the logo, tagline, and mascots but also by the quality of the programming and the alignment of the programs with the mission and vision.

What's in a Name?

Rebranding not only the new department but also the three major facilities was a real leap of faith. This conservative, traditional department once known primarily for sports was embarking on a complete change of not only the name of the department but also that of the Summit Community Pool, the Summit Municipal Golf Course, and the Summit Recreation Center. I expected some pushback from longtime residents, and push they did.

First, the Logo

I first planned for the layers needed for revamping the brand of the department. We would need a new logo, stationery, signage, promotional materials, taglines, uniforms, and official colors. But how could we translate this expanded vision and mission into one logo? It was a huge challenge. How could a symbol show who we are, what we do, and whom we serve? Can a logo translate into the concepts of reliability, honesty, and service? The solution to what seemed impossible came to us from our residents. All we had to do was read and listen to their comments:

- I love summer camp!
- Look, Daddy, I can swim!
- You're never too old to learn how to dance!
- The dance was a blast!
- The teen peer mentors were great with my child!
- Six hundred kids are playing basketball!
- I got a hole in one!
- Look, Mom, I got a trophy!
- Today I learned to ride a pony!

The recurring theme was excitement, and the symbol was the exclamation point. A logo was born.

How About a Tagline?

The logo was established, and now we needed a tagline and our unique selling proposition, or USP. The Summit Recreation Center had become the center of a controversy involving the Summit Senior Club. Promises made to the club had created a belief that the recreation center was only for kids, and the seniors felt they needed their own facility. Without the resources for or interest in creating age-segregated facilities, our mission was focused on making all the facilities available for all ages, creating an intergenerational approach to service delivery. From that mission came the "Share the Fun! USP," as well as a secondary USP, "Where Community Thrives."

These two taglines summed up the mission of the department: "We strive to be the place where all of Summit comes together to play, regardless of age, sex, race, religion, income, or ability." They tell the story that in Summit, "we share the parks, we share the buildings, we share the golf course, we share the pools, and we share the fun! In turn, Summit will thrive!"

Revamping Continues

I share this experience to show the layers needed to create the new brand for the department. In turn, the three main facilities in the park system needed revamping to match the excitement of the new brand and the focus of the redesigned department.

(continued)

From Summit Board of Recreation to Summit Community Programs—The Birth of a Brand

(continued)

The Summit Recreation Center became the Summit Community Center. The new name allowed a more comprehensive approach to serving the entire community, not just the sports enthusiasts. This change was not well received overall, but with time and explanation, the residents came to understand the change. Most of the community had grown up with the Rec, and the generation before them knew it as the Edison Recreation Center. How could they accept a new name? We communicated the need for the change and the intention to expand the facility to one that would serve all. Ultimately, the plan worked, and we are currently preparing for a $5 million expansion of the facility to allow for both shared and dedicated spaces.

So, if the Summit Community Center were to have its third name change in almost 60 years, why not the Summit Community Pool and Summit Municipal Golf Course? I'll share more about the mascots and sign plans that complemented these new brands later in the book.

The Summit Community Pool carried that name for nearly 40 years, but the facility had been renovated and the new direction of the department had made the pool into so much more. In addition, the Summit Community Pool had no logo or tagline for all those years. The name Family Aquatic Center would connote much more than just aquatics. A logo showing the new colorful umbrellas, the tree-lined hills, and the beautiful flowers of the facility has become the symbol for the Family Aquatic Center for almost an entire generation. New logos, uniforms, signage, and mascots turned this popular facility into the "hottest place to cool off!" in the city.

The Summit Municipal Golf Course was the first nine-hole executive municipal course in New Jersey. The golf course never had a logo or brand. The new name came once again from listening to the membership. Countless members came to the office and referred to the course as "the Muni." After hearing this hundreds of times, I challenged my staff to call the facility what it was commonly known as. The lightbulb seemed to go off for all who were asked. A new logo, tagline, and mascot followed. The Muni is now known as the gem of the park system!

A Rose by Any Other Name Would Smell as Sweet

In William Shakespeare's play *Romeo and Juliet*, when Juliet says "A rose by any other name would smell as sweet," she argues that it doesn't matter that Romeo is from the house of Montague, her family's rival. Just because his last name is Montague doesn't mean he is like the rest of the Montague family. This quote suggests that the names of things do not affect what they are or represent. Just because you change the name of your aquatic facility, it doesn't mean it is any different in the eyes of the customer. Real change must happen. When the name of your water park carries a negative connotation, then a name change and brand revamping are just the beginning. What do you do to restart the energy or reinvent your facility after a disaster or bad reputation?

New Jersey's Action Park is an interesting example of a name changed not once but twice. Once known as a water park with one of the highest incidents of accidents and deaths, Action Park was seen as a high-energy park that not only experienced a high number of accidents but also allowed out-of-control group rentals and some in-park violent behavior. It attracted teens and young adults craving high energy and adventure rides and attractions. With more reported incidents, the family market dropped off and the young-adult visitors increased. The name of the park became Traction Park, both in the industry and the media. How do you recover from that?

The park was sold and the name changed to Mountain Creek. The branding plan was directed at the family market and complemented the ski area and growing residential and time-share population. Several years passed, and a new group took ownership of the water park. As a surprise to all, the new owners not only returned to the name Action Park but also embraced its tough, high-energy reputation. The impact was high, with coverage on television and radio. Stories of the old park and its dangerous rides and group incidents were not only remembered but embraced in the oddest way possible. The immediate value of a return to and embracing of the negative brand perception was huge, but if it can survive is yet to be seen.

Turning around the legacy of the original brand will be a monumental task, and I question the approach. Recently, the State of New Jersey closed several rides at Action Park due to the high incidence of accidents. The old name has returned, and so have the reputation and record. It's interesting that the management at Mountain Creek turned that reputation around only for the new owners to return to the Action Park brand. The jury is still out on their decision.

Most of us in this industry will not face a challenge as daunting as Action Park, but aquatics does have implied risks in the delivery of service, and tragedy can result in the loss of life. If a facility has a reputation for a poor safety record, a tragedy will only complicate this reputation. In the swift response of social media, the facts are often lost while the gossip remains. A new brand in this case will have to portray both a totally new image and a focus on safety in programs, activities, and public relations. You don't have to create a new brand, but it certainly can rebuild the energy and acceptance of the facility. Be clear with your new message following a tragedy. Accept that the incident happened, and be transparent about the improvements made, whether or not you completely change the brand. Identify your weakness, be honest about your changes, and embrace your new brand.

How to Rebuild Brand Trust

How you deal with a negative image is one thing, but it is just as important to listen to your members. Let them vent their concerns, and listen carefully in this period of rebuilding. Certainly, trying to preempt bad customer experiences is the best practice, but when you have lost your members' trust, it is hard to win it back. Though longtime members are more likely to stay loyal than those who joined more recently, losing any members is a step backward and one you want to avoid.

Respond swiftly to members' feedback. Reinforce your changes and that the brand can be trusted. If you make changes that are not perceived as positive, you could even lose long-term members' trust. If you don't listen and respond responsibly, you will see your membership decline, and it may be too late to get those members back.

If the community has lost trust in the aquatic center, you have to be honest and acknowledge the issue with your members. The first step in rebuilding trust in any relationship is to say that you understand there is a problem, and you are focused on fixing it. If maintenance was an issue, acknowledge it and show the steps you have taken to improve the conditions. Not only make the changes, but communicate that you have done so. Reassure members that you want to know what *they* want, not what you think. Share their comments with your staff members. Let them hear from the customers and read the comments so they understand that the concerns are real and direct from the membership. This will make the members' concerns more real to the employees involved.

Themes on a Budget

For years, designers and operators of aquatic centers never thought about themes. In fact, the municipal pool environment was quite barren and institutional, with the exception of some grassy areas and limited plantings. Concrete was everywhere, and most things were painted a swimming-pool blue, if they were painted at all. Chairs and seating areas weren't much different than park benches. Private swim clubs had a bit more style in the 1960s and 1970s with the use of shade pavilions and awnings. Fencing was usually galvanized chain link, with the occasional board-on-board fencing for private clubs. The addition of multiple pools, the public's exposure to resort pools and amusement parks, and the growth in the water-park industry seemed to trigger the desire to be more than a concrete wasteland with a body of water inside. As zero-depth entries and lazy rivers made their mark in the municipal market, along came the concept of theming, and there was no turning back for the aquatic industry.

Don't get too anxious about budgets; this book is designed specifically for aquatic centers on tight budgets with little to no extras allowed. Theming doesn't have to cost tons of cash if done with a creative eye, some imagination, and a willingness to take chances. In fact, developing a theme and finding innovative ways to make it happen can energize your facility and your own outlook on the daily grind. There's nothing like a challenge to put a spark in your personal work and create a new environment for an aging facility. Of course, the best time to develop the theme is during the development of the branding strategy, but it doesn't have to happen that way. It can be exciting to breathe new life into an aquatic facility with a theme that makes it feel new again. The best thing about theming an existing facility is that you can do it in manageable, fundable steps that create excitement when members wonder, "What will they add next?"

Getting Started

Much like your branding strategy, you need to determine what theme best fits your facility and its mission. Working with the surrounding area can make this task much more manageable. If you are lucky enough to be surrounded by trees and a natural environment, it's a no-brainer to use a woodland theme. If your facility is a blue hole in the ground surrounded by concrete, you have a long way to go, but you do have an empty canvas on which to create your theme. If you are deep in the heart of an urban environment and you want members and guests to feel whisked away to an oasis, then tropical is a good bet. I've seen facilities beautifully themed with the simple and affordable use of annuals, potted flowers, and colorful banners. It may not be the theme that amusement parks are made of, but it will create a sense of arriving at a destination. All of these enhancements increase the perceived value of your membership or daily fee.

Take a look around your region and see if you can find a theme that best represents your area. Even history can become a theme. If your community played an important role in the Revolutionary War, why not create a theme honoring that past? In this case, your signage should follow a colonial shape to contribute to the theme. Add a lobby filled with historical photos and facts plus a mascot dressed as a Revolutionary War general, and you're on your way.

The city of Kokomo, Indiana, created a surfing theme with the most unlikely mascot: a surfing bull. You might wonder how a theme with a surfing bull could make any sense at all. But if you're from Kokomo, you know why! It seems that Kokomo's claim to fame at one time was having the world's largest steer. You might remember a scene from *Band of Brothers*, a WWII miniseries based on real life, where some GIs were arguing over which state had the largest steer. To prove a point, the soldier from Indiana had a sister at home who posed near the famous bull and sent the photo to her brother, who hung the photo in his locker. This story put Kokomo on the map, and the scene in *Band of Brothers* marked its place in history. The bull was stuffed and now sits in a park in Kokomo in a glass case, with the story behind the photo proudly displayed. On opening day of Kokomo Beach, the bull was taken from the case; dressed in a giant Hawaiian shirt, lei, and lifeguard whistle; and rolled on wheels to the grand opening ceremony. The young sister in the bathing suit, now a woman of advanced age, also appeared at the event and posed again for photos near the famous bull. That bull is now the centerpiece of Kokomo Beach and helped create the surfing theme. Small surfboards were used to name the events (an industry term for attractions), and the unusual local theme was a huge success.

Courtesy of Gretchen Masterfano.

From World's Largest Bull to World's Only Surfing Bull.

Aquatic centers in farming communities or western regions can have a lot of fun creating themes on a budget, because items that can be used in planting beds, sign beds, and entrances are plentiful. Auctions, estate sales, and even restaurant liquidations are prime sources for themes on a budget. The master at this is government-owned Hyland Hills Water World in Colorado, which uses found nautical items throughout the park, from fishing nets to floats and buoys. They camouflage fences in tube areas and place cannons in flower beds. The underground lazy river has a story line that an excavation explosion created the underground river, so they sank a front-end loader into the area to legitimize the theme.

Name That Event

Should you be lucky enough to have an aquatic facility with multiple pools, one way to get a big-park feel is to name each of the events. There are two ways to go about this naming process. The first and safest way is for you or your staff to name the attractions. This ensures you will be consistent with your theme and meet your goal for creating a themed environment. Or, you can take a risk and have a naming contest for each attraction. This can get your membership excited and garner some press coverage. Be sure to set all the parameters ahead of time. If you're aiming for a patriotic theme, let the contestants know the time period and the vision you have. Remember to reserve the right to not use any names that are inappropriate or don't match the theme.

Do you want a tropical, high-energy theme? Words like *hurricane* and *wild waves* work in that type of environment. If you are in the Midwest and have high-energy rides, *twister* and *tornado* might fit the bill. Is surfing your thing? Then why not use *wipeout*, *hang ten*, and *kowabunga drop*?

If you do choose to name your attractions, you have to believe in the names. Use them when training lifeguards and giving directions to patrons. Make them part of your vocabulary at work to help to create the mystique of your theme. Be sure to match your event names, theme, and sign materials to make it all come together. Using driftwood and rope on a nautical sign makes a big difference. Surfboards used as signs for a surfing theme make the theme believable. A vehicle from the time period of your theme would be a great addition; if not available all the time, consider using local vintage car clubs for a special event to draw attention and bring in new people.

Themes: The Light Version

Perhaps you are excited about theming your facility, but you just can't get your advisory board to go for it. There are still ways to create a theme based on some of the simplest concepts. For example, you can create the illusion of an English garden without going to extremes. White picket fences with flower beds will still provide a country feel

With a bit of imagination, even the most mundane buildings can become an attraction.

and charm. Include some garden items that can be purchased in any local garden shop or farmer's market. Do you have maintenance buildings with no personality? Create window frames and flower boxes, and those unsightly filter buildings are now quaint little cottages. Better yet, have your mascot peeking out the window. Now you've really created something from nothing!

The least expensive but most dramatic tool in your theming arsenal is fabric. It can camouflage unsightly areas, distract the eye from a huge sea of parking spaces, or fill in the high ceilings of an old bathhouse.

Ready-made banners with waves and aquatic themes are readily available from sign manufacturers and banner companies. Bolts of fabric purchased from craft shops and remnants from local upholstery shops can provide the same effect. Don't go spending money on pipes and permanent anchors; use your flower beds instead. A simple green temporary fence post covered with PVC pipe and a little Velcro can turn fabric and pipe into a beautiful themed enhancement. Think about strapping these pipes and banners to existing fence posts and voilà! You've created excitement.

I was fortunate to manage the Summit Family Aquatic Center, known as the proud home of the Summit Sharks. When rebranding this renovated facility, I knew that the community was not ready for an in-your-face theme. The logo of the facility highlighted the shade structures, the surrounding hills, and my favorite flower, the morning glory. This subtle yet effective theme was very well received.

With a desire to do more, I challenged myself with finding a way to incorporate sharks into the facility in addition to Shark Diddy, the mascot. When traveling along a country road in New Jersey, I saw a display of wooden sculptures of animals that had been carved using a chain-saw, beautifully done and very affordable. I then set out on a mission to add a new shark sculpture to every flower bed in the facility on a shoestring budget. Worried about getting those purchase orders approved for something like a chain-saw sculpture of a shark? I hear you! It's a three-dimensional promotional item, as far as I'm concerned. And it worked! But how to add a different type of shark each year became the challenge. I was able to find local and regional artists who worked in all types of media, from fiberglass to metal. Searching the Internet, I found a variety of decorative sharks appropriate for outdoor use and slowly and methodically added them to the facility. From finds in craft magazines to online finds from artists around the world, I became intimately aware of shark art everywhere I traveled. With each addition, we dedicated the piece to one of our partners in safety. Each unveiling was an experience and brought in the families of those honored. From our emergency medical services (EMS) to our fire, police, and public works departments, all were touched by the gesture and came out in large numbers to support our efforts. A shark sculpture garden in a municipal aquatic center: That's an award-winning concept on a budget.

What if you need a focal point that makes a statement? One low-budget idea is to ask public works to provide large rocks from another project and place one in each flower bed. Large rocks make great backgrounds for words, slogans, or logos and fill out a flower bed nicely. They also make excellent photo ops and selfie backgrounds.

For the Heck of It

Sometimes themed events are put there just for the heck of it. Here are some examples that add fun and value to a facility at little to no cost.

- Add warning signs for alligator crossings, or signs that say, "Don't feed the sharks!" Each little gesture makes a theme statement.
- Make a library corner with the local library for a book and magazine exchange. Put a small awning over the books and create a quiet space for reading. It provides a valuable service and creates an enhanced experience. How about a time-out area? Complete with stroller parking, you can create a space within an aquatic center where overly excited little ones can go to calm down and have quiet time with Mom or Dad.

- How about plywood cutout boards that match your theme? The cutout allows guests to stick their heads through and have a fun photo op.
- Name a playground area after someone from the city's history and have a sign explaining who the person is and why the playground is named for her. How about a sign in a playground area that states, "Caution: Future World Leaders at Play"?
- Do you have an area where kids queue up for a slide or ride? What better way to get them into the spirit than with trivia signs, pirate maps, wildlife stories, and other items that match your theme and are educational?

Themes don't have to be as elaborate as a pirate with a talking parrot on his shoulder to be effective. Once you catch the theming bug, you won't be able to stop!

Lessons Learned

- A name change alone cannot renew confidence in your brand. You have to earn it.
- Rebranding an existing facility in a community can get emotional. Be respectful of the history.
- When rebranding because the facility has had an incident or has developed a bad reputation, admit to the issue, talk about how it's been corrected, and own it. The rest will follow.
- Share the process with your staff, and be sure they buy into the new brand. It has to be a 100 percent effort to get your membership on board.
- Branding takes time and is a multilayered approach. A name change alone never works.
- Themes can be subtle but still make a difference.
- Listen to your customers; their language can help you to create the new brand. Listen more and talk less.
- Use auction items to fill in flower beds and entrance areas.
- One person's junk is another's treasure. Dumpster dive if you must.
- Use large rocks, tree stumps, and other things found in nature.
- Create areas that can provide quiet time for kids and parents.
- Themes have to be coordinated with your branding plan in order to be effective.

2

CREATE BRAND VISIBILITY

Now that you've done the hard work of establishing your brand, tagline, and promotional materials, there are still layers of work that need to be built. Incorporating the brand throughout your facility in an effective and attractive manner opens up many possibilities as long as you keep those creative juices flowing. Most places cannot afford a total rehab or addition of new attractions, but they can ignite excitement by incorporating their brand in every aspect of the facilities and programming.

Post Effective Signage

Signage is an important part of any aquatic facility in order to meet codes and regulate behavior, but when done correctly it can also be an integral part of your operation and reinforce your brand. With a little effort and creativity, signage can be fun and add excitement to the atmosphere of the facility.

Guidance on signage is usually found in the state bathing or amusement code. You can also find helpful recommendations at the Centers for Disease Control and Prevention (CDC) website (www.cdc.gov/healthywater/swimming/materials/posters.html). While visiting facilities that you enjoy and find attractive, study the signage design. Take notice of signs you think are effective and focus on their colors, lettering, style, and location.

The optimal time to create a sign plan is when you are first designing a facility. But, there is no reason you can't design a side plan that can be retrofitted to the facility and done in phases when budget is a consideration. In this chapter, I'll share some of the best and worst signage I've seen in the industry and offer tips on how to create an effective sign plan without breaking the bank.

If money is no object (which is seldom the case), you can work with a graphic designer and sign manufacturer. Or, you can take some of my suggestions to save money and become a better consumer of sign materials.

Planning Your Signage

If you've done your homework and developed your brand identity as covered in chapter 1, you've already established the following things you will need to create your sign plan.

- Color scheme
- Theme
- Fonts
- Logo
- Mascot
- Facility name
- Characters

Consider naming each area or amenity. Naming your lazy river, slide complex, children's pool, and other attractions will add fun and whimsy to the facility and sign plan. In the early stages of an aquatic facility design, think about sign placement in flower beds, entrances and exits, fences, posts, and entry facilities. Where will the guests view the rules? Will you need a measuring stick at the base of the slides to document required heights? Will you need exit directions at the base of a slide or next to a landing pool to meet local codes and control throughput on a ride? Will you include the sign plan in the construction budget? Will signs be included in your design specifications?

Budgeting

Before you start to worry, there is never enough funding for the dream sign plan! Quality signage is much more expensive than you might think. That's why preparation and study are necessary if this is your first adventure in creating signs. When establishing your plan, remember to include setup charges, special-order charges, and labor costs. Architects who create elaborate sign plans for facilities that can afford it estimate the cost of signs to be 7/10 of 1 to 2 percent of the overall construction budget. Take a few minutes to figure that cost for your facility, and you'll be sure to give yourself enough time to get it right and at the right price.

The best way to save money on a sign plan and start to complement your brand is to standardize the size and shape of the signs. This technique helps avoid a haphazard look to the facility. Uniformity in signage also makes it much more effective and identifiable. The shape of the signs can add to the excitement and brand reinforcement.

Planning ahead will also help you select sign materials that are site specific. All this planning ahead will result in cost savings and an interesting and effective sign plan. Go shopping at your local sign manufacturer and learn the difference between a special-order fabric and a standard fabric. Learn about the thicknesses available. For signs that must be hung on a single or double post, make sure to select material that comes in a thicker fabric. If the sign will be hung on a wall and away at a distance, you can save on the signs by using a thinner material.

The variety of sign materials available today is huge and includes different approaches to achieve the same effect. For example, there are carved signs made with a foam product that will add dimension to your logo or your mascot's image on the sign. The same effect can be accomplished when the sign will be viewed in the distance by layering sign materials that are less expensive.

Is vandalism a potential problem for your facility? If so, be sure to pick the best materials that will minimize vandalism. Sign placement can also control the level of vandalism a sign will receive. For example, peel-and-stick vinyl is an affordable alternative for a sign giving instructions on the use of an amenity such as a slide. If you fail to put a protective coating on this type of sign and you place it along a queue line, it is almost guaranteed that bored teens waiting in a long line will remove or move vinyl peel-and-stick letters to turn the sign into a game of hangman. Your sign will be sure to read differently when they get done with it!

You also want to consider where the signs will be placed. Will the signs be indoors in high humidity? Will they be outside in the direct sun all year round or just for the summer season? When a facility is new or has added a new attraction, you may want to use a temporary material such as Coroplast. This is a plastic-covered cardboard-type material that is often used for temporary signs and is sold at a cheaper price point. Although sign manufacturers will tell you they are only temporary, they can last several years with care. Sometimes, it takes a year or two of operations before you truly know the rules needed for a new area or attraction, and Coroplast provides the most flexibility.

Be sure you are matching your logo and color scheme with a color that is not a special order with the sign manufacturer. Any color can be special ordered, but at what price? Make sure your color scheme is available in a standard color and that your sign manufacturer will keep it on hand.

Determine the shape of your signs. Remember that special shapes can cause costs to rise. Keeping it simple is your best bet. Will you have rounded corners to avoid injuries, or will you stick to squares and rectangles?

If you take away anything from this chapter, it's the simplest but most effective hint: Simple borders can improve readability. The biggest bang for your buck is to include a simple border on any type of sign or poster. The border helps the eye focus on the message. Signs with borders read 26 percent faster than signs without borders. Another helpful hint is that information that is presented in a second color improves retention by 78 percent. Studies by the Pennsylvania School of Ophthalmology have proven these two concepts (Townsend 2008).

Be sure to understand the sizes your sign material comes in. You can save money by understanding the size available and try to design your sign plan to get the most cuts from the standard sign material by size. For example, if the material is available in pieces that are four by eight feet (122 by 244 cm), design your signs to get the most cuts out of that size of material. You'll save money by getting the most signs out of the stock material and minimizing waste.

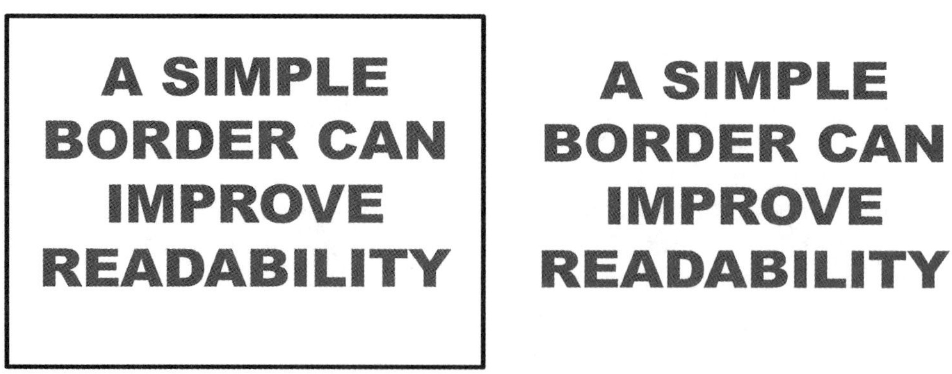

My favorite sign in a sign shop sums up the best advice on signage that I now live by.

If your rules could change, why not create a sign with a removable insert that can change without sacrificing the whole sign? You can create a sign with more expensive carved foam with a three-dimensional look, and add a thin PVC sign featuring the rules.

New facility, lousy signs. Temporary doesn't mean awful!

Your budget is the determining factor when selecting sign materials. We would all love to have three-dimensional carved signs with the best materials, but if you can save money and still have an effective sign plan, wouldn't you rather spend the money on other items in your facility? I know I would.

Next to no money available for your signs? Thanks to computers and color printers, you can make attractive temporary signs until your budget allows for more permanent signs. A simple laminating machine can help you create temporary signs as long as they are attractive and follow my suggestions for design. Just be sure that they are neat, hold up in the weather, and are friendly to your guests. If not, they will cheapen your facility and give the impression that you don't care.

Unique Sign Options

An often unused billboard space is lifeguard and staff shirts. Why not deliver a message to guests on the backs of your safety staff? "I'm watching your child. You should be too!" is on all of the lifeguard shirts at the Summit Family Aquatic Center. The campaign is part of our parental responsibility signage to remind parents of their role in watching their children.

Meaning of Colors

Signage is an essential method of communication around the world. The layout, images, and colors make signs recognizable at a glance and can help create memories. Have fun with it! Colors make an impact. Each can be used to invoke emotions or actions. It's interesting to see how certain colors appeal to certain people. We often select the wrong colors when painting a room for children or perhaps our kitchen. When the sex of a baby is not known, the parents will paint the room yellow. However, this may not be a wise choice because yellow could excite a baby and not be conducive to sleep. Want to lose a few pounds? Paint the lightbulb in your refrigerator blue. The blue light will make almost everything in the refrigerator look blue and unappetizing. So, whatever you do, avoid blue on your kitchen walls.

Red—The most powerful color demands attention and action. Heat, anger, passion, and dignity are associated with this color. It is often used to excite appetites or behavior.

Blue—The second most powerful color stands for wisdom and strength. It is the most politically correct of all colors and seen as neutral. It is most associated with intelligence.

Yellow—This is the color most visible to the human eye. It is lively, stimulating, and vibrant. It draws attention.

Green—Universal for nature, this color represents freedom and peace. Only use white text on green background, not green on white, because it is easier to read. Green is often hard for people to read, so use a different color for instructions or promotional text.

Safety Signs and Colors

When developing safety signs for mechanical and maintenance areas, not only are the colors of the signs significant, but so are the shapes. These signs or stickers are usually found on mechanical equipment along with arrows that show the direction of liquids.

Red—Round in shape with black images or text on a white background. Red should be at least 35 percent of the sign. A red sign indicates danger or inappropriate behavior or tells people to stop.

Yellow or amber—Triangular in shape with black images or text on a yellow background. Yellow should be at least 50 percent of the sign. Yellow signs are used for a potential threat such as wet floors.

Blue—Circular in shape with white images or text on a blue background. Blue should be at least 50 percent of the sign. Blue signs are used for obligatory instructions such as parking.

Green—Rectangular or square with white images or text on a green background. Green should be at least 50 percent of the sign. Green is used to highlight importance, such as for a first aid sign.

Fonts

The top fonts for signs are effective and remain popular today. Have you selected the font that is best for your brand? It's best to stick to the following list of tried-and-true fonts; those that are trendier can show the age of a facility, just like the wrong color selection. Always use one font throughout your sign plan. Consistency in font and color is imperative to reinforcing your brand.

1. Helvetica (60+ years old)
2. Futura (90+ years old)
3. Garamond 500+ years old)
4. Bodoni (200+ years old)

As you develop the wording for each sign, you must determine how the sign will be used. This will help you select the size of the text (see table 2.1). Black, red, and white text is best read from a distance. Readable distance can vary 10 percent between colors. Bold fonts with significant spacing are the most effective. When developing signs for interior retail

TABLE 2.1 Letter Visibility Chart

Letter Height	Maximum Impact Distance	Maximum Readable Distance
3 inches	30 feet	100 feet
4 inches	40 feet	150 feet
6 inches	60 feet	200 feet
8 inches	80 feet	350 feet
9 inches	90 feet	400 feet
10 inches	100 feet	450 feet
12 inches	120 feet	525 feet
15 inches	150 feet	630 feet
18 inches	180 feet	750 feet
24 inches	240 feet	1000 feet
30 inches	300 feet	1250 feet
36 inches	360 feet	1500 feet
42 inches	420 feet	1750 feet
48 inches	480 feet	2000 feet
54 inches	540 feet	2250 feet
60 inches	600 feet	2500 feet

This is based on dark text on a plain white background in clear weather conditions. There is an approximate 10% variance when using various color combinations.

Note: 1 inch=2.5 cm; 1 foot=.3 m.

locations, one to two inches (3-8 cm) is the recommended size of the text. Outdoor banners should have text no smaller than three inches (8 cm) and should be readable within 30 to 100 feet (9-30 m). If you are having trouble sizing your text, rely on these tips or your sign manufacturer's guidance. What does your font say about your facility?

Sign Quantity

Your signs should complement your facility and aid in guest satisfaction, but there are many schools of thought about the appropriate number of signs. Many of us feel assaulted by signs everywhere we go. Having the right amount of signage, meeting required codes for aquatic facilities, and not creating sign litter can be difficult. In an aquatic facility, the other challenge is maintaining lines of sight for lifeguards and staff. Will guests be able to read the signs while sitting in the hot tub? Remember that when signs compete against each other, no one message dominates, which can confuse your guests. If rules signs are too long, guests will not read them. Many facilities only use signs that are required by their state and then complement them with symbols, especially when there may be a second language in the community.

The sign size should fit the environment. Signs need to be easily read but not overpowering. They should be placed at eye level. Use short bullet points and keep it simple. I love to use water droplets instead of dots or dashes when listing rules. It adds some fun to an otherwise boring sign and helps build the brand. Be sure to state the facts and only the facts, but be friendly when possible. Try to limit the number of times you say the word *no* or your facility will seem unfriendly; instead of *no*, perhaps use words like *you should know* or *please*. At the bottom of the sign, be sure to put *Thank you*! These simple tips will make your signage much more friendly.

Why Spelling Matters

As I travel the United States consulting with aquatic centers of all types, I'm still shocked at the number of signs that have misspelled words and bad grammar. With spell-checker programs, this is totally unacceptable. A simple misspelled word can deliver a very different message. When accepting signs from your manufacturer, have several people review the signs to make sure the message is properly spelled and understandable.

Gotta Have a Gimmick!

Brand identification is very connected to the unspoken word. Your logo is so important to your brand that it should appear on all of your signage. This is simple to do if you create a template for each sign so that the design is consistent and continues to reinforce the brand. Placing a simple wave, flower, or splash in one corner and your logo in the opposite corner is a simple way to establish a format for the entire sign plan. Is the logo recognizable without any words? Can you repeat it while still delivering your message on each sign? Absolutely!

The Summit Department of Community Programs in Summit, New Jersey, has an exceptional branding plan that revolves around a simple symbol: the exclamation point. The exclamation point is recognizable and can be duplicated easily and affordably in foam, wood, plastic, and even inflatables. It connotes excitement. It's simple but delivers a big message.

Crystal Springs Family Waterpark in East Brunswick, New Jersey, turned a brackish swimming pond into a sparkling pool. The secondary message was that the aquatic center was the gem of the park system. So what inexpensive gimmicks made their sign plan sizzle? Each sign was painted in the official colors and finished with a silica clear coat that shines in the sun. The idea of crystal-clear water was reinforced inexpensively with the sparkling crystal effect. It was affordable with a big impact.

Not every sign plan has to rival Disneyland. Sometimes the simplest sign plan is all about colors and shapes. The materials can also vary from plywood or pieces of plastic cut in different shapes and layered to look like building blocks or Lego bricks. Brilliant!

Sometimes signs are effective when they are included in a sign plan just for fun. Signs indicating stroller parking or a quiet zone for babies create areas that add to the value of the guest experience.

Specific Signs to Post

In the aquatic environment, the rule that is seldom required by code but is the most important is, "Don't drink the water!" If you want to keep guests safe from waterborne illness, this sign is imperative. Certainly, behavior signs such as no diving, no running, and so on are vital, but signs discouraging prolonged breath holding have also become important at all aquatic facilities.

Entrance Signs

Do you welcome guests at the entrance to your facility? From the moment they enter the parking lot, do they identify your brand? There are simple ways to welcome guests, create a sense of arrival, and begin the experience without breaking the bank. Architecturally, your design team can use a variety of techniques to welcome guests, including decorative fencing, display boards, planters, and of course signage. Fencing can feel welcoming or restrictive. Fencing that is black and vertical can disappear from the eye. In the aquatic design, be sure to provide a peek-a-boo effect with your fence material. You want to provide privacy for guests while they are in the aquatic center while also providing enough visual space for passersby or potential visitors to get a peek at what is in store. If your fencing isn't welcoming, then it is important to include a welcome sign and a sense of entrance for guests. This can be accomplished in a variety of ways.

Flower beds with surplus equipment that matches your brand can be attractive and enticing. Have a facility with a barn or farm theme? Why not use farm equipment as decorative items in a flower bed? Go to auctions, look for donations, and get free used and broken equipment that can add some pizazz at your entrance. How about animal characters from chain-saw artists? They can add both fun and fantasy on a budget!

Murals are the least expensive way to create a sense of arrival and can create a huge impact. Consider working with local talent, including high school and college artists, to keep your costs down. With Google Images and the ability to project images with overhead projectors, murals are much easier to create. Entry buildings and older bathhouses can be transformed with a mural or signage that is layered for a sense of depth. Today, most sign manufacturers have the ability to wrap entire buildings, desks, and kiosks. This can make a building look new with wrapping that can be either permanent or temporary.

Indoor aquatic centers often have foyers that are made of cinder block and have an institutional feel. That can easily be remedied with several types of inexpensive applications. Do you have historical photos of the facility? Guests would love to see them in the bathhouse or foyer. Why not use them as a history lesson while covering up ugly old walls? Or, how about hanging children's art from mobiles? In Cranford, New Jersey, the Cranford Community Center has strung the tops of all types of plastic containers, creating colorful, environmentally friendly mobiles that fill the air with color and movement. A little bit of recyclable material and a lot of creativity fills the facility with whimsy.

The area outside the facility where guests line up for admission is an opportunity to reinforce your brand, advertise your programs, and make guests feel welcome. There are inexpensive, temporary signs that can be changed daily. Use them effectively by adding air and water temperature, thoughts for the day, advertisements for events, and just a friendly hello!

Why not create a four-sided sign that mimics your shade structure? A four-sided sign allows the foot traffic to spread out, offers multiple surfaces for announcements, and gives guests something to do while they wait.

Some of my favorite entrance signs at an aquatic center are weather updates warning guests when there is a chance for inclement weather.

What a great service for guests, and it helps the guest services staff get through a difficult day. Signs that show operating hours and rides that are not currently in operation will at least notify guests before they purchase tickets exactly what value they will be getting that day.

At NRH$_2$O in Texas, they have a sandwich sign that states when there is especially high attendance and recommends that guests may want to visit another day. Brilliant! Sandwich signs offer great flexibility, especially when you need to redirect foot traffic or close an area of the park. They are affordable, interchangeable, and neat. Directional signs and "You Are Here!" boards are necessary in large parks. Directions, a map, a clock, and a thermometer are great additions to directional signs. A sandwich board on wheels that can be wheeled out on big attendance days is a practical answer to entry signage or snack-bar menus.

Are you proud of your swim team? Create a sign that spans the entrance of the facility to announce this, such as "Proud Home of the Summit Sharks!" You'll promote your swim team, encourage respect and honor for the team, and fill an otherwise vacant space with color and excitement.

Often bathhouses are drab and unexciting. Most are made from block and painted with a high-gloss paint once a century. Why not use some inexpensive PVC sign material to create tiles to decorate the walls? You don't have to retile the entire bathhouse; just add some color, flowers, or logo tiles to break up those huge block walls. Paint a stripe along the walls that leads to the exit doors. Simple painted lines and geometric designs can give new life to an old bathhouse.

As aquatic managers, we are always looking at the interior of our facility. We see the facility every day, and we tend to not see what a new guest would notice. Ask friends or colleagues from another facility to visit. Tell them to be honest, and you can do the same for them. A fresh set of eyes can identify areas that need attention.

Sit inside your facility and look outside. What do guests see? Perhaps you need to clean up the back of the house. Are your dumpsters unattractive? Do guests see them when they arrive? Perhaps a new fence is necessary. Or, why not decorate the fence or paint a mural to make unsightly items more attractive? Key West, Florida, has done this well by having local artists decorate dumpsters, barricades, and electrical boxes throughout the city. The artists sign their work and add to the local flavor. You can do that too!

In East Brunswick, New Jersey, a train trestle is outside the family aquatic center. An Eagle Scout painted the trestle and improved its look for his project. Now when guests set their chairs to look away from the action, the view is much more pleasing. Some things may not be in your facility, but they still reflect on your brand.

Themes make signage much more friendly!

Measuring Sticks

Measuring sticks are required at facilities with slides that have a height requirement. It's a perfect opportunity to incorporate your mascot into the sign plan. I like using a measuring stick in the design because children understand the idea of reaching the marking on the stick. Be careful in planning for these measuring instruments, though. You have to be sure there are no sharp areas that children could walk into and injure themselves. I've seen some that are done well and others that are downright frightening. The most important thing is to make sure they are installed on an even surface and to the proper height. I once gave loose instructions to a maintenance employee who installed the stick well above the actual height. A child would have had to be six feet (2 m) tall to ride that slide!

Look Up!

Sometimes signage is most effective when it draws the eye up. A client of mine was adding attractions over the years and couldn't understand why one particular pool was not getting the use it had before the new additions. It turned out that new guests to the facility could not see the older pool because the line of sight was obstructed. By creating an archway with a bright, colorful sign bearing name of the attraction, use increased considerably. Sometimes it's not the attraction that's the problem; it's that the guests can't see the attraction, or there is no sense of arrival.

One of the least expensive ways to add color and distract guests from the asphalt jungles that are parking lots is fabric. Banners are inexpensive and can draw guests' attention. Moving fabric, whether in parking lots, at entrances, or in flower beds, can give the impression there is a breeze on the property and can add a little excitement.

Municipal Signs

There is no more dreaded sign than the political signage often required at a construction site at a municipal or government facility. Even with tight budgets, you are often required to spend a big piece of the signage budget on a sign that states the elected officials involved with the new facility. Unless you are required to use a standardized sign on all projects, why not make the most of it? During the construction of Crystal Springs, we had to have a sign that said "Coming Soon" and listed the names of the elected officials who voted on the project. With some clever thinking and thoughtful design, we were able to use the sign prior to the opening and then remove the names of the elected officials, resulting in a sign on a major road welcoming guests into the park.

Historical Signs

I used to hate purchasing expensive brass plaques to mark the year of construction of a facility and the elected officials involved. Quality brass plaques can cost thousands of dollars. But, project after project, I would bite the bullet and purchase the required plaque. I changed my mind about brass plaques when, after creating a wildly successful aquatic facility, my job was eliminated following an election. Now, I'm glad I purchased that plaque and embedded it in a large rock at the site. Every time someone walks by that plaque, they see my name, and it makes my heart soar. You might find that including similar types of signs offers a bit of history about the facility and gives officials, benefactors, or patrons something to be proud of that encourages them to continue to support the facility.

Departure Signs

Earlier in this chapter we talked about saying hello and welcoming our guests. As they drive into the parking lot, do they feel welcome? With proper planning, you can create a two-sided sign that says "Welcome" as they enter and "Thanks and Come Again!" on the reverse side. You can save some cash by making the sign two sided, and make friends as they come and go!

Mascots as Community Icons

Who doesn't enjoy visiting an amusement park and coming home with a picture of a favorite character? Who hasn't attended a sporting event and laughed at the antics of the team mascot? Who hasn't purchased a product because they took the word of a fuzzy creature or a cute talking bunny? We all have!

Mascots are one of the most visible branding vehicles at your disposal. They have a universal appeal that has existed for years, and the origin of the word is traced back to Provence and Gascony, France. It was meant to describe an object that would bring good luck, such as a lucky charm or a talisman. It was introduced to the English language in the late 1800s.

Merriam-Webster defines *mascot* as, "a person, animal, or object adopted by a group as a symbolic figure, especially to bring them good luck." Traditionally, mascots have been used to represent groups with a common identity, such as schools, teams, military units, or brand names. In addition to the original intent of brand recognition, they have also served the marketing profession as spokespersons, or spokes-creatures, so to speak, for consumer products that have spun off into merchandise and other revenue sources.

Costumed mascots are common in the amusement industry and usually serve as goodwill ambassadors in the community. They are not as common in the municipal aquatic environment, but they can have a remarkable impact on the perceived value of the guest experience at aquatic facilities of all sizes.

Why Have a Mascot?

People love to meet mascots, have pictures taken with them, and give them a hug or a high five. They are an excellent way to market your brand without breaking the budget. They can get people excited about your aquatic center or water park, reinforce your theme, and put some punch into your marketing plan. If you want to bring attention to your aquatic facility and make it stand out in the crowd of choices people have in deciding how to spend their leisure dollars, developing a mascot may be the most affordable part of your marketing plan—and it can also infuse fun into the facility. Of course, the mascot is not the only component of a successful strategy, but it will certainly be the most memorable.

How do mascots amplify your brand? They are more than just fuzzy creatures that appeal to kids; they often become even bigger than the brand they represent. The right choice of mascot can translate into merchandise sales and access to other forms of media and promotion, resulting in a positive bottom line.

The right mascot can open many doors. Mascots create an emotional experience or connection with guests that is difficult to create under other circumstances. When chosen carefully, they are funny and approachable and find affection from kids and adults of all ages. They turn the aquatic experience into something people care about and identify with.

Using a mascot in promotional campaigns and in social media helps get attention of your target audience at first glance. Mascots are one of the most effective advertising tools. They have been able to deliver messages—even those that are serious, such as Smokey Bear's messages about forest fires. Mascots are also able to represent your facility where advertising may not be welcome, such as in a classroom. Because of the entertaining nature of a costumed mascot, you may have access to children at a school festival where traditional advertising is not allowed.

When considering an animal or human mascot, remember that animal mascots are effective because most people both young and old find cute animals charming. Animal mascots are especially relatable when they have human features, behaviors, and clothing. The most important thing in choosing your mascot is to give it a personality and let it grow with your facility.

A mascot should become synonymous with your message and shed a positive light on your facility and mission. Remember that your mascot is an extension of your facility, your staff, and *you*! Make the right choice and manage it well, and you will create not only a mascot but a community icon.

How to Choose the Right Mascot

Some mascots simply choose themselves, while others may choose you. Sound ridiculous? Not so. You may get lucky, as I did when branding an existing aquatic facility that had long been the home of the Summit Sharks. In this case, it seemed the mascot simply chose itself! For example, as you prepare to design and build a new facility, perhaps you realize that the area is home to a certain type of frog. Or, maybe your mascot symbolizes a local or regional concept such as a historical area, coastal region, or mining community.

Successful mascots don't have to be cartoon characters. For example, staff members at an aquatic facility shot a promotional video that gathered lots of attention on Facebook and YouTube. The next thing we knew, the duo went viral and unintentionally became local media darlings. A word of caution when developing mascots who are real people: If those staff members leave, there goes your video campaign, and you are without a popular symbol of your facility. With a costumed character, you can always find someone else to wear the costume.

If you find that your choice of mascot has become wildly popular, be sure to purchase another identical costume or at least another head in case one is lost or the costume becomes unavailable later. If you identify and build a campaign around your mascot and the costume changes, or it is lost or is no longer available, it could be disastrous and expensive.

If this is your first time facing the challenge of incorporating a mascot into your marketing strategy, you may wonder how you can justify spending money on a mascot. Will the community embrace this new character? Who will wear the costume? Can we afford it?

Haven't we all purchased a display ad in a local newspaper or online news site? You bet we have! The cost of incorporating a mascot into a facility or department is equal to the cost of a one-time display ad in many areas. But that ad only gets seen once and has a limited impact. Think of your mascot costume as a four-dimensional ad or sign, and there is your justification for a purchase that will be associated with your facility for years to come.

Still not sure you can afford a mascot? Do an online search for generic mascot costumes and then personalize them yourself with uniform shirts, a Hawaiian shirt, or a straw hat. You can do it on a shoestring budget of about $500. Custom costumes can be expensive and range in the thousands of dollars. More generic costumes with quality construction such as fans in the head range between $1,500 and $2,500. Just be sure to do it well, or don't do it all. You can purchase costumes online through the amusement industry suppliers or have them made locally at a costume shop. If you have a talented seamstress in your community, you may be able to design and construct the body of the mascot locally and only purchase the head through a costumer.

The tiny town of Ringwood, New Jersey, took a look at its sociodemographic factors. Ringwood has some rural areas and is home to a beautiful state park, so the area is heavily wooded. Residents decided that a wildlife and nature theme would be the best bet.

They considered a fox—too scary.

They considered a skunk—too smelly.

They considered a buck—too pointy.

They considered a squirrel—too nutty.

Their final choice was a bear. A friendly, happy, huggable bear it was! You'll find out his name later in this chapter.

Whenever possible, you should consider your mascot when you are developing your brand or rebranding an existing facility. The colors, theme, and mascot should all relate. In the case of the home of the Summit Sharks, the Summit Community Pool had always been the home of the Summit Sharks Swim Team. In 2007, the decision to rebrand the facility as the Summit Family Aquatic Center was made because of a new design and a new approach to aquatic programming. As part of the rebranding process, the decision to use a shark as the mascot was an easy one, but what would it look like, and how would it translate with children? This is not always an easy task. Some kids are afraid of everything; there are kids who are afraid of clowns and Santa. So accept right now that your mascot will not charm everyone.

Choose the costume carefully to find the right mix of fantasy, reality, and acceptability. Make sure the costume or cartoon mirrors your message. Be careful of any stereotypes or potential cultural issues associated with your choice. Let's not forget that mascots in commercials and of sport teams have often been the subject of protest and debate. From the Taco Bell Chihuahua commercials of the 1990s to the Washington Redskins debate today, mascots do evoke emotion, but just how much and what kind depends on your choice.

Since you are choosing a mascot for an aquatic facility, consider whether your mascot can swim. A beautiful government-owned water park in Illinois had a farming theme with buildings designed to look like barns and farmhouses. Situated where cornfields once stood, it seemed like a perfect idea, and it is still successful today. But when it came to choosing a mascot, they chose a chicken. Last time I checked, chickens don't swim! They countered the chicken stereotype by putting the chicken in an inner tube. I don't know about you, but do you want to hug a wet chicken?

So, back to the shark in Summit. When settling on a mascot, another effective marketing tool is to develop a name and backstory for the mascot. Why would a shark be at an aquatic center? What's his story? Where did he come from? Why does he have feet? We had to develop the reason for the Summit Family Aquatic Center shark. Of course, he could be the head lifeguard and teach kids how to be safe in and around the water. This may seem counterintuitive for a shark, but it's an ironic backstory that continues to grow today. Creating a backstory and sticking to it in all of your events and marketing pieces elevates the importance of the mascot and drives up the appeal. By sticking to the backstory, it was easy to continue the legend of this friendly shark that soon became a community icon. He's so recognizable by residents that no one is shocked to see the shark in parades, on video, at city council meetings, and anywhere people congregate in the city.

When the mascot comes out for an appearance, we announce a shark sighting over the loudspeaker. We've developed a story line that has the shark returning to Summit every summer from wintering in Australia. That has helped us explain to children why he is in town all summer and not seen as often in the winter. The more his backstory develops, the greater his value and impact on the community as well as the aquatic facility and its members. This all translates into positive acceptance and support of the facility and its mission. What's this shark's name? Why, it's Shark Diddy, of course! You'll hear later how this came about.

Shark Diddy doesn't just strut his stuff in Summit, but he takes every opportunity to visit with other state mascots at their events. He goes to Slider the Otter's birthday bash at Seaside Height's Breakwater Beach water park. He runs the bases at the Somerset Patriots' baseball stadium with their mascot Sparky, and he has challenged the Montclair State University Hawk to the ALS Ice Bucket Challenge. In exchange, when Shark Diddy throws a party, they all attend.

Shark Diddy isn't the only fuzzy icon in Summit. With his success, it isn't a surprise that the municipal golf course developed a mascot. Because golf is linked to Scotland, the course chose McMuni as their mascot: a happy Scottish terrier with a tartan hat and sash. With his own little set of clubs, he's a young golfer's favorite. He guards the golf course and makes it fun. He makes appearances along with Shark Diddy at major events, and then he reigns over his own events for photo ops with golfers at outings and special events. The annual PAL Fishing Derby is one of his favorite events because he meets the entire community there. McMuni, like Shark Diddy, does lots of education in his role as mascot. McMuni helps kids understand the rules and occasionally chases the geese that populate the course. He is represented as a cartoon character, appears in lots of videos, and is a social media darling as well.

In Ringwood, New Jersey, their bear mascot also has a story. It is folklore that he found his way out of the woods to join in on the fun he heard coming from the borough hall because he wanted to be part of the excitement. The kids of Ringwood know the story and love it. Ringo the bear shows up at sporting events and events sponsored by other agencies. He has been featured on social media such as Facebook and Twitter. He ran a 5K, participated in trunk or treat for Halloween, and is the star of movie night. He visits the schools and even welcomes Santa to town for the annual parade. According to staff members, Ringo is the best investment dollar for dollar that they ever made for marketing and promotion.

When picking a mascot on a tight budget, do some Internet shopping. If you hope to match your mascot to your theme and potentially create affordable merchandise and promotional items, you want to pick an animal or character that is readily available in plush or plastic. Search Google Images to see who else is using your idea and how it has been received by the public. Investigate how the mascot managed and merchandised by others, and learn from their victories and failures.

A small municipal water park in Lafayette Indiana was under design. The city had adopted the tropical theme and named the park Tropicanoe

Cove (see page 9 for more about this facility). Despite my protest, they chose a catfish as their mascot—a bottom-feeding freshwater fish! Because they didn't think it through, they now had a disconnect between a catfish and the tropics. Who ever wanted to hug a catfish, other than those folks who go catfish-hole diving in the South? The other problem was finding plush and plastic catfish items: They would have to be custom ordered, and that doesn't do the revenue or expense picture much good. The catfish may be one of my least favorite mascots ever.

When choosing your mascot, be sure it translates well to print media. You will want to incorporate your mascot into your sign plan. Does the image look OK in black-and-white print? Is it cost effective to produce in color? Be careful not to finalize your cartoon before you translate it into fabric. On paper, this small drawing may be charming. In person and six feet (2 m) tall, it may be ominous and scary. Approach with caution! Ask yourself the same questions about your mascot that you did for signage (see page 27). Early planning will lead to the right choices and an affordable result.

It is possible to create interest and a sense of whimsy by having your mascot only in cartoon form. For example, Crystal Springs Family Aquatic Center hasn't fully embraced the mascot concept, but it does use cute characters throughout the facility with a natural theme. Otter and duck cartoons are used on measuring sticks, signs, and promotional materials. In Kirkwood, Missouri, the Recreation Station has a railroad theme since it is located near an old railroad station. The measuring stick is a train conductor cartoon, and he is visible throughout the park. One day, should they want to elaborate on the conductor, a costume with a head could be created or a volunteer conductor could wear clothing, similar to the cartoon. In Twinsburg, Ohio, home of the annual twins' convention and parade, the mascots are an adorable set of cartoon twins who grace the signs throughout the park. This makes perfect sense in Twinsburg: It marries a local tradition and capitalizes on an already-famous concept. Getting human twins to play the mascots may be a challenge, but certainly twin costumes complete with heads could be derived from the original artwork.

A question I am often asked is whether a mascot must match the logo of an aquatic center. The answer is no. Think about how colleges and universities select their mascots. It doesn't have to reflect the name of the institution, but it should have a connection to the message you are trying to deliver. If the connection between the facility and the mascot has to be explained, then perhaps you need to rethink your direction. If the image isn't easily identified and associated with your facility, it needs more exploration.

Naming Your Mascot

Some facilities choose to create excitement by having a contest to name their mascot. This approach has its merits, but tread lightly. Be sure to set the rules of the contest and reserve the right to refuse all entries. Remember that a mascot is a commitment of time, money, and reputation. In many cases, mascot names are catchy and easy to rhyme, which is important when thinking about promotions and theme songs. Some names are directly related to the mascot, such as Sharkey for a shark. And some of the most memorable mascot names make no sense at all. They come about through staff meetings, brainstorming sessions, or divine intervention. Shark Diddy was named about the same time that rap mogul Sean Combs was changing his name to P. Diddy. Shark Diddy just rolled off my tongue one day, and it felt so right. The rest is Summit history!

Rules of Engagement

Be sure to establish rules of engagement for your mascot at appearances and at all times in the public eye. It's vital to their success and survival. Following are some rules to consider for mascots.

- Never speak unless the character is human. Once a mascot speaks, you will have to replicate that same voice to maintain the magic. Even the major theme parks do not allow their costumed mascots to speak for this very reason.
- You should always have an escort. A mascot needs an assistant because of all the attention received. Vision is compromised and footing can be challenging. The escort can speak for you and help you avoid embarrassing situations.
- Keep your head on your shoulders. Most mascot costumes have an arm harness that attaches the head to the costume. Always have your arms through the harness so a quick action or fall doesn't cause your head to come off and expose your identity.
- Always enter with a big announcement. Pick a theme song or introduction and stick with it. Make every entrance a big one. Tease the audience and make them feel the excitement of the entrance.
- Get down to kids' eye level when possible. Be aware of your size. When visiting with kids, kneel, bend down, or sit when possible. Be careful not to be eye to eye with them if they can see into the costume head. It can break the fantasy if they see a human inside. They'll try everything to prove you're not real.

- Beware of little boys! Little boys seem to react the most aggressively to mascots and want desperately to be dominant in the exchange. Many have a tendency to pull tails, kick, punch, and grab. It may be a natural desire to be dominant or to deal with their fear of the character, but it can get ugly in the wrong atmosphere.
- Never approach a crying baby or cringing adult. When you see a baby crying, turn away and approach carefully. Signal to a parent if it is OK to advance.
- Never lend out the suit. Your mascot's reputation can easily be discredited if you lend out the costume. You never know where the costume could appear and what they might do in it. Consider the mascot costume as part of your brand or reputation. Are you willing to put everything you worked for at risk?
- Behave in a manner that protects the brand. Mascots should always be polite, unassuming, and gentle while in character. The behavior reflects on your brand.
- Do not let an empty suit be seen. Don't destroy the fantasy. An empty suit can ruin the mystique that you worked so hard to create.
- Understand your power. When a mascot has been well developed, be aware of the attraction of the image and use it to your facility's advantage.
- Make larger-than-life movements. Exaggerate every move.
- Always think about the photo op. Take some test pictures and find the best postures for your mascot. Does the head need to be turned for the best view of the face? Do you lose the view of both eyes if the head isn't turned?
- Pose in a big way. Stand in front of a logo and repeat whenever possible. Stand near attractive backgrounds, not garbage cans or maintenance areas.
- Wear the brand or enhance the costume for each occasion. If you're having a superhero party, does your mascot wear a cape? If pirates are the theme, can the costume include an earring, boots, and an eye patch?
- Create a signature dance move. Strike a pose and make it work. Learn a simple dance and do it when you are happy. Learn a pose that expresses sadness. Your body language counts when you are a costumed mascot.
- Use hand signals to communicate. Your hands can speak for you and help you through any event.

- Work in short intervals even if you have an internal fan or cooling vest. It gets hot in there.
- Ask for permission to visit. Don't go into a store, bank, or office without receiving permission. Costumes can be threatening in a bank, for example, if a six-foot (3 m) shark isn't expected that day.
- Conserve energy when possible. With time, you will become more and more comfortable in costume and understand your limitations. That's the advantage of using the same person in costume when possible.

Caring for Your Mascot Costume

Your manufacturer will have specific instructions for your particular costume. Be sure to follow them precisely. Use a fabric spray immediately after use to keep the costume as fresh as possible. Pack it away in a container that can breathe. Some folks add a dryer sheet when it is packed away to help to keep it fresh. Never put it away wet! Store the costume in a cool, dry area where it is not visible to young children. You don't want to ruin the fantasy. You may also want to work with a local costume shop to refurbish your suit annually.

Always have the containers clearly marked if you separate the head from the body. In Summit, we have both Shark Diddy and McMuni. While preparing for a big event at the Summit Family Aquatic Center, a young programmer grabbed two containers without looking in, gambling that they were properly marked. When getting Shark Diddy ready for a big reveal, we opened the containers and found two heads. In this case, two heads were not better than one! Needless to say, we laugh about it today, but it was not so funny that night!

Size does matter when it comes to selecting your mascot costume. Is it too large to easily transport to and from events? How will you conceal it? Will you be able to put it on while in a van or a small space?

Here's an example: Some colleagues were excited about buying a costume for a starfish mascot. They got caught up in the look of the costume and the entertainment value of the design, but they never thought of transport. They now own a fabulous costume that they can't ship to and from trade shows due to the size, because the costume doesn't break down into smaller pieces. Research the care and storage of your costume before you make the investment.

The next generation of costumes is the inflatable suit. This holds lots of possibilities for those under a tight budget. Production costs will be lower, but will the suit hold up over time? The answer is yet to be seen.

Mascots Gone Wrong

There are occasions when a mascot can go wrong. What you see in the catalogue or what your graphic designer has created sometimes does not translate to a full-sized character. What was cute can quickly turn threatening. Be sure to choose a mascot that is unique and relatable in order to relate to the widest audience. When used as a measuring stick, pointed ears, tails, and whiskers can become dangerous. A large costume with poor sight lines can become a hazard for tripping and falling. Additionally, small children may not only be frightened, but they also can be knocked over and overwhelmed.

When getting people excited about a mascot's appearance, be careful to not get them too excited. Large crowds and an exciting mascot can create a need for crowd control. Mascots have a way of getting folks excited. You may need barricades or a separate entrance and exit for your mascot's quick retreat.

Be especially careful as you select your mascot. While searching for a Scottie-dog costume online, we couldn't find a ready-made option that fit that name. We then commissioned a custom costume only to find that the online costume company had a Scottish terrier that was exactly what we were looking for at a far better price. But, the mistake didn't end there.

Once our custom Scottie dog, McMuni, made his appearance at our golf course, we realized that his dark hair, face, and eyes made him almost indistinguishable in photos. And isn't it all about the photo? We ultimately did a test makeover on McMuni and used paint to give him white eyebrows and a white mustache. After some practice photos, we had what we always wanted: a Scottish terrier that was photogenic. Live and learn!

Who Wears the Suit?

Professional teams and collegiate mascots select their talent through auditions. Mascot training camps and videos are also available. Being a mascot is a developed talent and does get easier with time and commitment. Whenever possible, training one or two staff members or volunteers to wear the costume is ideal. It will make for a consistent show with each appearance. People will come to expect certain behaviors from your mascot.

Some aquatic centers have seasonal personnel serve as their mascot. That works well. Seek out dance, drama, and gymnastics talent because they understand performance. Your mascot is part of your brand, but it is also entertainment. Consider having tryouts and recruit local talent. It can be a fun volunteer experience or a fun summer job. Don't be surprised if the shy type becomes a whole new persona when in the costume. It brings out the inner child in many people and allows them to be someone else. The costume serves as a disguise for a closeted entertainer.

At the Summit Family Aquatic Center, we would ask for volunteers from the staff to become Shark Diddy. We had mixed success from season to season depending on how much interest was expressed by seasonal personnel. Just before a big themed event, our volunteer didn't show up. The presiding officer of the advisory board asked what was happening. When we told him we were short one staffer to appear as Shark Diddy, he offered to help, and three years later, we can't get him out of the suit. He dons that suit and he *is* Shark Diddy. He has embraced this role as his alter ego, and we have been extremely fortunate to have him be our Diddy. He cares for the costume, sews a new outfit for each year's themed events, and makes appearances.

Because your mascot comes into direct contact with children in the facility, they should pass any background checks required by any other employee who works with children. You must protect your brand. The mascot's behavior at events and respect for the costume and the brand should be carefully supervised. Mascots can make or break your brand should they lose patience or embarrass the organization.

Make Your Mascot a Rock Star

Once you have elevated your mascot's image in the community, there is no telling where it may turn up. Every opportunity where potential members congregate is an opportunity to promote your brand. Explore opportunities that fit your brand's message. Visit the library at story time and suggest books on sharks or sea creatures. Send your mascot to visit the locations of corporate sponsors. Offer your mascot for opening ceremonies of local sport organizations. Have your mascot march in parades or judge the belly-flop contest. Send your mascot to the mayor's retirement party, the farmers market, or a local charity event. Hold a raffle for your mascot to attend a child's birthday party. The possibilities are endless; just make the most of each appearance by bringing along coupons, promotional items, and free passes.

Be sure to include your mascot on promotional items to increase its visibility. The Summit Family Aquatic Center has collectable pins featuring Shark Diddy, and sharks are included in every promotional gift basket donated to charitable efforts. He's included on all signage and lifeguard shirts, and he's memorialized in wooden statues in planting beds throughout the facility.

Consider producing a documentary about your mascot's backstory. Or, how about featuring your mascot in your public service messages?

Shark Diddy's story line has him wintering in Australia and swimming to New Jersey for the summer months. We track his journey back to Summit on Facebook to start the excitement growing. He's even got his own Facebook page and has had an online blog as well. Marketing interns love these assignments and provide a refreshing sense of humor to the marketing of your mascot.

Each year, the theme for the Summit Family Aquatic Center is built around Shark Diddy. Whether it's Shark Diddy's Birthday Bash, a Wild West Summer or Superhero Summer, or a Yo Ho Ho Pirate Bash, each event features Shark Diddy as the focus. He leads the annual float parade, and when the season draws to an end, he leaves the Diddy Dive-In Movie to return to Australia. There is not a dry eye in the house as the kids wave goodbye to him. Shark Diddy is not just a mascot; he is a community icon.

Lessons Learned

- Give yourself plenty of time to research the signage materials available in your area.
- A simple border improves readability.
- Signs with borders are read faster than signs without borders.
- Information presented in a second color improves message retention.
- Learn the psychology of color and the industry standards for mechanical areas.
- Helvetica and Futura are the two top fonts used.
- Two heads are better than one: Always have a spare mascot head. The body of the costume can often be recreated.
- Beware of boys! Some may be aggressive with mascots.
- Never put away a mascot costume in a closed container.
- Always send your mascot with an escort or handler. Mascots should never be alone.
- Be sure your choice of mascot translates to a relatable full-sized version.
- Mascots should practice photo poses for the best outcome.
- Mascots are not just for kids; adults love them too. They can evoke authentic emotion in your membership.

PART II

MARKET DEVELOPMENT

Courtesy of Sophie Mannaerts.

3

BUILD COMMUNITY CONSENSUS

Courtesy of Gretchen Masterfano.

Whether you are hoping to build a municipal aquatic facility or you are a private developer seeking approval for a new commercial water park or attraction, developing community consensus and support for your project is the first step to your ultimate success. Adopting the "If I build it, they will come" approach is a sure way to fail when conceptualizing a new facility. Even if you have done your due diligence and completed a financial feasibility study, concept renderings, and all the marketing and promotional materials, you still need to build community support to ensure the facility's future financial success.

Do Your Homework

To be successful, you have to understand that there are many factors that could influence support for your project that have little to do with the project itself. You need to be aware of other city projects and priorities as you start building community consensus for your project. Read and learn everything you can about your community that could create opposition to your project. Is there a conflicting issue in the neighborhood where the new or improved facility is located? Perhaps there has recently been an environmental concern over water usage in your state. You either have to be prepared to address the issue with facts and figures or introduce the project at another time. Become familiar with the local planning and zoning board's latest project reviews, and learn the board members' sensibilities. You'll likely appear before them to justify your project, so familiarity with their priorities and statutory responsibilities is key.

Don't underestimate NIMBY, which stands for **n**ot **i**n **m**y **b**ack**y**ard! No matter how great your project is, remember that neighborhood opposition can be a highly emotional issue that has caused the demise of many proposed projects. Sure, you may think that would never happen in your community, but one angry misinformed neighbor can stall and even end your project before it begins. Accept that the process involves both real and perceived issues. The frustrating thing is that opponents don't have to be accurate; they only have to be loud. You, on the other hand, must have the facts and figures to support the need for the project and its benefits to the community. I've worked on so many community consensus campaigns over the years for both public and private owners, and it never ceases to amaze me what can cause the failure of a project. I have seen citizen action groups formed with every acronym possible, including CAVE People—Citizens Against Virtually Everything!

What is behind the NIMBY mentality? I've heard every argument in the book, including parking concerns, noise, costs, scholarship aid, environmental issues, "it's an amusement park," and the list goes on. Sadly, it often is driven by fear, and in my experience, many of these fears are veiled prejudices. Fears about nonresidents, bussing of "those people," and other disturbing concepts have been used to put a stop to public facilities that will enhance and engage the community. Try to learn that language if it exists around your project, and be prepared to address it throughout the process.

Be aware of any recent issues locally or nationally that involved a water park, a drowning at a public facility, a pool chemical leak, or a riot at an amusement park. They may have nothing to do with your project, but they will be cited by the opposition and used to your disadvantage.

Check your terminology and understand its impact. Aquatic centers today come in many shapes and sizes. Who would think that the choice of wording could jeopardize the outcome of your project's acceptance by the community? I've seen it happen.

The industry has seen many changes over the years, with the introduction of amenities such as zero-depth entry, lazy rivers, water play, splash pads, slides, and wave generation. Although these are all quite common now in public facilities, they conjure up visions of amusement parks and water parks for those not familiar with these concepts. Calling your project a *water park* may evoke emotions about parking, traffic, buses, noise, and amusements. If this is the case, depending on the size of the project and local sensitivities, calling your project a *family aquatic center* might be the safer choice of the two.

Six Phases of a Public Project

I've worked on dozens of projects all over the United States and have found that every project has the same six phases:

1. *Enthusiasm*—Everyone is excited when a project begins: staff, elected officials, and residents.
2. *Disillusionment*—Reality begins to set in as costs become real, problems arise, and the project is not as easy as everyone thought.
3. *Panic*—All projects meet with delays and timelines that are tight and seem unmanageable. This is when directors start to wonder if they will make it through the project to its opening day.
4. *Search for the guilty*—If things get delayed or costs rise, government entities start looking to blame someone. It's usually the person who introduced the concept.
5. *Punishment of the innocent*—You may have no control over problems that arise, but you just might get the blame.
6. *Praise and honors for the nonparticipants*—The very politician who was publicly against the project will be the one who claims the credit at the opening ceremony or wants to be the first to ride the slide.

I've traveled throughout the United States assisting communities and commercial developers through their projects, and I have observed each and every one of these no matter where I've been!

Within the industry, there are those who state their protocols for how to describe a facility. If it has a lazy river or moving water, it's a water park. If it has flat water, it's an aquatic center. If it has flat water and a combination of interactive and traditional amenities, it's a family aquatic center. I don't buy any of that. Call it what works for you and your situation.

Selling the Public Project

Imagine a sign at a public construction site that reads, "On this site, the government will get us into another fine mess." You may not think that way, but many residents do. There is a general distrust of local government and its ability to get a project done on time. Think about the news stories about NASA and their $1,000 toilet seat. Before news went viral, that news story was quoted for years when a public project was proposed.

An editorial cartoon ran in an Indiana newspaper when Tropicanoe Cove was about to open in Lafayette. It featured two kids and their mom at the entrance to the water park, with the mom saying, "Remember, we're Democrats. Try not to smile or look like you are having a good time!" Don't underestimate the power of local politics. Your plans for success could become a political football. Educating the public about the benefits of the new facility, knowing the finances, and having your facts in order is the only way to battle the politics of success. Many directors and managers have met their demise through the political approval process on a project, even though the project moved forward and was ultimately successful. The best way to prevent this is to not be the face of the project. Instead, train a team of people on the facts and figures so they can help educate the public about the project and defend it if needed.

Why a Referendum?

In some states, a referendum is required for a major project such as funding a new municipal water park. You can't escape a mandatory referendum. Many of the steps to ensure the successful passage of a referendum are similar to those of public education and consensus-building campaigns, but if a referendum can be avoided, I highly recommend the latter process.

When a public referendum or public ballot question is not required by law, it often has proven to be a stall tactic. It could be a thinly veiled lack of political courage or leadership. You'll hear politicians and opponents call for a public referendum on the project, hoping it will fail. Many factors outside the actual details of the project can cause a failed referendum, and that's often why opponents to the project ask for it. Anything from ballot question positioning to conflicts with other ballot questions to voter apathy can cause the end of a project. Once a referendum fails on a project like a public aquatic facility, opponents and political leaders will remind you of the loss forever, making future projects difficult to propose. The referendum can be fatal.

Why Not a Referendum?

In my experience, there are many reasons why you should avoid a referendum when trying to take the pulse of the community about your project. With a ballot question, you only get a yes or no from the voting public. You rarely get to understand the reasons behind the opposition to your project. Was it the cost? Was it the location? Was it a cultural issue? Anyone who offers an answer is purely speculating. With a community education and consensus-building program, you can get the feedback you need to scale the project, change something about the project that doesn't work in the community, or abandon the project altogether. The public will tell you much more than a yes or no vote. Once the answer is no on a referendum, it tends to stay that way.

The wording of a referendum can also be responsible for negative outcomes. Oftentimes, word count is limited and the referendum is written by the law office, not by the aquatic supervisor or marketing department. People need simple terms that they understand. When voters find it difficult to read or comprehend a ballot question, they choose no. Whatever you do, don't combine questions. There's nothing more dangerous than bundling projects in one referendum. The public sees it as wild spending. Use the KISS technique: **K**eep **i**t **s**imple, **s**tupid. Timing is everything in planning for a new or improved aquatic center. By the time a referendum makes the ballot, is it on a date with traditionally poor voter turnout? Is it placed with several other spending bills? Both of those conditions can be poisonous to a positive outcome.

Project opponents have the freedom to spread negative or inaccurate comments in the community with no restrictions; however, many of us in government positions are forbidden by law to spend money or time or share personal opinions on a referendum. The best bet to fight the opposition is to form a nonprofit friends group that can raise money and enter the political fight. Unfortunately, most people think parks, playgrounds, and aquatic centers are great improvements, and they are sure the government will do the right thing, so they don't feel as motivated to go out and vote. I've had many experiences following a failed referendum when people call me, shocked that it didn't pass. When I ask if they voted, they almost always say they didn't think their vote would be needed. Encourage every supporter to vote for your project!

When explaining why someone should support your project, provide not only the facts about the project but also highlight its local economic impact. It's about so much more than the daily rate at the gate. Use graphics and statistics that matter to the public and the business community. Years ago in Toledo, Ohio, there was a referendum for a levy for a stadium and aquatic center. The focus of the educational pieces was that it was about more than just the numbers; it was about taking pride in the community. They compared Toledo to other communities with similar facilities and the revitalization that the projects would bring. They presented the facts that the project would mean more than just a stadium and a water park: It would boost the local economy by providing 930 temporary jobs, $28 million in wages, $84 million in local spending, and 420 long-term jobs, all for a sales tax levy of quarter of a penny. They focused on the sales tax not being related to groceries, rent, mortgages, and other key points to residents, pointing out that 25 percent of the levy would be paid by visitors and 30 percent of the stadium cost would be paid by state and private funds.

The referendum failed, even with great statistics, promotional materials, and public forums. The water park was added to the referendum to sweeten the stadium concept for the public, but bundling the two in an effort to get the referendum passed ultimately worked against them. The voters, who could not separate the two projects, voted no. When the water park never materialized, residents wanted to know where and when the water park would be built. They thought they had voted against the stadium and assumed the water park would still happen. Lesson learned? Quality facts, figures, and promotion couldn't compete with the bundling of two major projects, and the opposition to the stadium outweighed the desire for the water park.

Remember that lack of trust in the government is often the end to a referendum. If the public doesn't believe your facts or have confidence that you can get the project done and keep it successful, a referendum is negative. In addition, there is a growing fear of increased taxes with each and every new parks and recreation improvement. Once considered one of the most important priorities in city government, overburdened taxpayers want to cut the fat, so to speak, while we work against issues like obesity. It may not make sense, but be prepared for an uphill battle.

Why Not a Nonbinding Referendum?

A nonbinding referendum is like being almost pregnant—it is a weak political attempt to gauge the interest of the community without binding the community to it. If the vote is yes, the local political body can still decide to say no. Lots of work will be done for a nonbinding referendum, and there is no definitive outcome. You are better off spending

Referendum Tips for Success

- Remember that no public money can be used to sell the referendum.
- Form a friends committee and let them sell the project.
- Only the committee can raise funds; you can advise, but stay away.
- Use quality materials for promotion.
- Train a stable of speakers to keep the message consistent.
- Request ballot placement as soon as possible in order to secure a good position.
- Be sure of the political timing.
- Watch the wording of the referendum.
- Never combine projects in the referendum question.
- Don't ignore the grassroots opposition; it is stronger than you think.
- Don't depend on the local press, because they could turn on you.

your time educating the community, gauging community consensus, and building support.

How About a Survey?

Communities that don't need a referendum often think a survey will give enough feedback on a project to determine its direction. I only wish it were that simple. Depending on your budget, you can choose to go with a reputable firm to conduct a survey by phone, text, Internet, or paper. For those with no budget or more modest means, the Internet offers easy and affordable survey processes. Whether you go high price, high tech, or do it yourself, a survey document without the proper format, questions, and education piece can squash your project.

Valid surveys can be helpful because they can measure community interest on a wide variety of topics. Surveys can provide feedback on activities, features, pricing, use, and geographic and age-related interests. This will not only serve you well as a survey document but will also help you in the design of your project. Surveys may prove or disprove your facts, but they can certainly help you understand if the public has received your message. Surveys are a good way to get attention for your project, but they do not guarantee its success. A survey of the general public will certainly get the conversation going and the press interested. Be sure to use a survey document early on in your process. It's hard to stay objective, but it is extremely important to not sway the voting.

A scientifically conducted survey can result in a confidence level of 95 percent with a 5 percent margin of error. A small community can consider 300 to 400 participants as successful, midsized communities should try for 500 to 600 respondents, and larger communities may need closer to 1,000 to be valid. The participants should reflect the demographics of the community. The beauty of funding a professional survey is that is can be viewed as an independent opinion and therefore carries more political clout.

Most online, affordable surveys are rather short and not as scientifically valid. They also allow for ballot stuffing, and surveys that don't have controls on how many times someone can respond or can't be restricted to taxpayers could backfire on you. Especially for these types of surveys, craft the questions carefully. In addition, if you ask questions without a community education campaign, you may not get the answers you hope for.

You work within the aquatic environment, so you are familiar with aquatic center amenities. However, many survey participants may not understand their function. People who are unfamiliar with today's aquatic centers may hear the phrase *zero-depth entry* and assume it refers to something in an amusement park, is expensive, or is unnecessary. If they know that this amenity allows people with limitations to enter a pool with dignity and confidence, they may answer your survey questions differently. Keep in mind that people only answer from their frame of reference.

Although you may get positive results to the question of whether or not the community would support the new facility, surveys do not guarantee the viability of the project in the long run. Often people vote affirmatively on a survey, but once prices are posted or the facility is unveiled, they

Turning a Survey From Bad to Good

During a public education campaign and consensus-building process for Crystal Springs Family Aquatic Waterpark in East Brunswick, New Jersey, a local paper decided to do a small survey among its readership. It asked several questions without the benefit of any educational piece and claimed that it was an independent survey of readers. The real intention was to not support the project, which was the first of its kind in the region and a high-profile political argument. Determined to put the project to rest, the headline read "Only 500 Families Would Join Crystal Springs!" What could have been a public relations nightmare turned into celebration when the aquatic facility took out an ad in a rival paper, declaring that the facility only needed the support of 400 families to open.

are not ready to show you the money! Although a survey can be part of an overall public education campaign and consensus-building process, it should never stand alone as the final word on how the community has spoken. Surveys are most effective when used as a design tool or as an avenue for public input.

What's the Alternate Route?

The alternate route can be taken at any budget level and has been the most successful in my work in the industry. Whether done by a professional communications firm or in house on a tight budget, the components of a successful public education and community consensus-building process are the same.

Although staff may have been involved in the evolution of a project from concept to financial feasibility studies, the public education and community consensus campaign should be citizen driven as much as possible. A comprehensive public education campaign including a website and materials with frequently asked questions, photos of similar facilities, explanations of the amenities and who they serve, and financial information will be needed. Instead of adding a page to your already crowded website, a dedicated website is highly recommended. Allowing questions from the public through email, text, and phone will increase participation. Work with small focus groups, educate the stakeholders, and seek out the opposition in order to create a successful campaign. Allow visitors to your website to learn about the amenities, see those amenities in use in other facilities, and paint a picture of the activities to be offered at your center in order to obtain the most honest feedback.

In addition to the website, place information throughout the community for easy access. If people have limited Internet access, where can they see the data? Share information at city hall, the public library, and the businesses of supporters. Allowing input to be compiled in a way that can be presented to decision makers and easily understood by the community is vital. Use diagrams, graphs, and charts that are easy to understand. Make sure all promotional materials are good quality, because this reflects on the quality of the proposed facility.

Public education opportunities are crucial to the success of your initiative. To make this process manageable for you and your staff, gather a group of volunteers who can speak with one voice on the project. You could also create a video presentation to be shown at any public gathering possible. The video message will always be the same, and there is less possibility of bias and bad information being shared.

Public education sessions should be offered to all ages, neighborhoods, and service delivery areas. Print materials in multiple languages that match your community's diversity. Take advantage of every possible service-group meeting; the Rotary Club, Elks, and other service organizations are great places to gauge community support and distribute information. Why not take your aquatic center concepts to schools to gauge youth and family opinions? You'll find out some interesting things from your youngest potential customers. And remember that although Mom and Dad make the ultimate decisions, kids can certainly influence purchases.

Gathering input from both an online survey and community education sessions is imperative to your final analysis and report to decision makers. With local and regional television stations and other video options, live coverage of the education sessions allows residents to watch the presentations and react to the panel live via phone, email, text, and social media. These can be much easier and interactive forms of feedback than paper surveys!

Assure those who participate in surveys and educational sessions that their input will matter. When educating the community about my first large water-park project, we held public sessions and recorded the input. We also provided a paper document that folks could easily submit to share why they did or did not support the project. We also asked them about their most favorite amenity and their least favorite. We assured the residents that their input would be reviewed by the design team. This was a highly contested, highly emotional project. The completed park was the culmination of lots of hard work in educating and building public consensus. It still operates today and has kept its promises to the public.

Create a Study Committee

As part of a public education and consensus-building process, many communities have instituted study committees to spearhead this process. This approach is more time consuming but removes the professional staff as the face of the project. Staff can work behind the scenes to assist the study committee with facts and materials. Many of the suggestions provided earlier in this chapter will also serve a study committee well.

When forming a study committee, select representatives who reflect the demographics of the community. Don't stack the committee with only advocates for your project; balance the group with opponents. As they say, surround yourself with your enemies. You can hope to turn them around or at least learn why they oppose the project and prepare your counterarguments accordingly. Be sure to include representatives of the local governing body and mayor's appointments. Keep the study to an odd number for voting purposes. Limit the time for the study, and set a date for the final report. Otherwise, opponents of the project will wear the study committee down until they give up on the project. Make the study committee recommendations final and sunset, or they will go on forever. (Sunsetting a study means it has start and finish dates and will not go on forever.) Often, study groups are commissioned as a way to delay a difficult political decision. If you have start and end dates, it puts pressure on the governing body to make a decision.

In asking a study committee for a final consensus, allow the participants to have both a personal opinion and a group opinion. Publish all opinions in the final document. People are more careful with their words when they know their opinion will be public. You may wonder, why bother with the two positions? It's been my experience that the public process will influence the members, and they may support the project because of the public input even though personally they will not use it or support it. By asking for and sharing both group and personal opinions, the committee members have an opportunity to be heard; their opinion still matters and they can support the project with their own caveats. For example, someone may support the project but not if it is available to nonresidents. If you don't allow for this type of split opinion, you might only receive a yes or a no vote without knowing why. The reason for the vote is the important data.

Whether you choose one or all of the processes shared here, remember that the best approach to ignorance about a project is education. Make every public event an opportunity to educate, allow the public process to work, do your homework, and the reward will be a new facility for your community.

Turning Supporters Into Customers

If you are a public entity and have taken my advice so far to effectively create your brand and build community consensus, it's natural to think the job is done. After all, you have developed a large group of enthusiastic members of the community who are excited and looking forward to the new facility or the new addition to your aquatic center. But those of you who operate commercial aquatic venues can also benefit from this chapter. These tried-and-true practices can take those who support such a commercial enterprise as a beneficial addition to their community and turn them into paying members and clients.

These techniques can also turn around critics of your development project and turn them into informed potential supporters. The confidence you may have developed that those project supporters will naturally turn into members is naive. There's a big difference between supporting a public project and putting down your hard-earned money to become part of the new or improved facility. So many factors come into consideration when the public is considering a project. Many people will oppose a project because of outside factors such as their own priorities or political philosophies. Many will state their support for a project because it is the right thing to do—not necessarily for themselves but for the good of the population. Others will support or oppose a project because of political considerations such as the support of a candidate or party in power, not because they can't wait to swim in the new facility. Private developers of water parks, health clubs, and swim schools encounter many of these same issues. All politics are local, whether you are fighting for a public aquatic center or against a major commercial enterprise from fear of traffic, parking, and other issues that can become politically charged.

The major factor working against both the public and private sectors is the time that lapses between the approval process for a project and the project completion. How do you keep the energy flowing over several months or even years? In other chapters, I share the concept of making every step in the process an event. That certainly keeps the project alive, viable, and in front of the press and social media. But, how does that translate into supporters becoming members?

For the commercial swim school or aquatic venue, the time span from concept to opening day plays a pivotal role in the financial viability of the business. Failing to keep up the energy while awaiting approvals can be devastating and derail a project.

In other businesses, the cost of customer acquisition is a common topic around boardroom tables. It's no different for public projects. What will it cost for us to acquire new customers? How will we do it? Where will we focus our efforts? What can we afford in paid advertising, staff time, and social media? These are all things you should consider. The most important decision you will make as you prepare your customer acquisition plan is determining the best time to start the process. This is a delicate decision. It is extremely difficult to sell a facility before its completion.

Selling the Project Has Only Begun

The effort you put into turning supporters into members or acquiring members for your aquatic center or commercial project must be part of a strategic plan that is goal driven and well thought out. Without a plan in place, you will find yourself trying various strategies that have worked for your other programs or facilities in the past. But, selling a project that is not yet a reality is even more complicated. Today, consumers have so many choices when it comes to their leisure spending that selling a concept is that much harder. Once you have established your goals, you can then identify your methods, create your strategy for each target market, and determine the techniques you will use with each of those markets.

This will help you spend your resources in the most cost-effective way possible and ultimately sign up new members.

Who are trying to reach? Throughout the community consensus-building process, you most likely amassed a large contact list. These contacts are vital to the success of the project. And, don't disregard the sentiments of the opponents to the project. Include them in the process. It's better to be surrounded by your enemies, so you know how to combat their negativity. The greatest thrill is getting a project opponent to become a member! Then, my friend, you have hit a home run.

Who Is Your Primary Target?

Looking back at your financial feasibility report, who is the main target market from that study? Then look at that market and break it into subsections. Is it families with young children? Families with schoolchildren? Who is your secondary market to target? Is it senior citizens or empty nesters? Fitness swimmers or tourists? It's important to identify these targets because the techniques to reach each one can be very different. A well-executed financial feasibility report should do most of this work for you, including identifying your reach. Will you target these potential members within 5, 10, or 25 miles (8, 16, or 40 km) of your facility?

What Are Your Goals?

For both public and private projects, you must be sure your entire team knows the goals. Each and every member of the team, whether associated with the aquatic center or not, should be aware of your goals so they can encourage participation or at least refer an interested party in the right direction. So much of community-based recreation services is based on one customer at a time. Win over one customer and the rest will follow. This attitude needs to be part of the daily operation in order to be successful in selling a new project.

Set membership category goals, and share the team's progress throughout the process. Folks who find themselves in recreation and parks love challenges and competition. Keep track of the metrics involved with your goals for each category. This will help you understand where you are being effective and where you need to reset your priorities. If these goals are not shared, your marketing efforts will be scattered and unproductive. You need to spend your time and energy on acquiring new members, not necessarily selling to the current membership. Start to build your customer acquisition analytics from the very beginning. Track those who were involved with the community consensus process and see if those supporters have become members.

Make the groundbreaking memorable and fun by theming.

There are so many more platforms to use today than there were years ago. Social media plays a very important role in selling projects such as aquatic centers and there many tactics to use; we will cover those in chapter 8. One drawback of social media is that the attention span of potential customers is now severely limited. We need to use put energy toward the most efficient platforms and learn to get the message across quickly and succinctly. Focus on photos and emotion-based messages. Getting attention and turning that attention into action is the true talent in customer acquisition.

This is why strategy is so critical. For example, in trying to reach the senior citizen market, there may be two tactics to take. One tactic would be social media, which may not be the best approach with older adults. In this case, traditional press options should be considered. These nuances based on target markets make your strategic plan even more important. Be careful not to highlight every aspect of the new facility as a technique to reach your market. Focus on one major aspect, such as fitness swimming or quality family time, so as not to overwhelm the potential customer.

How Will You Reach Your Target?

Now that you've created your strategy and the techniques or tactics you will use to reach your targeted audiences, continue to keep an eye out for

Courtesy of Gretchen Masterfano.

Make your photos interesting to attract attention.

new strategies you could employ. Become an observer of what seems to work for others. Keep the list of techniques fresh and new. This is why keeping analytics is so vital to this process. Jettison the tactics that didn't work and be open to trying new ones to reach that market.

Conserving your energy is my best advice. If you've chosen this book as a tool to help you as a private entrepreneur or the director of a small to mid-sized public entity, you will benefit from its advice. Public or private, many aquatic operations do not have separate marketing divisions. Particularly with a new facility on the horizon, there will be plenty to get done in addition to your customer acquisition plan. When the energy is high for the project, you are filled with ideas and want to focus on every target market. Pace yourself and focus on one target and one tactic at a time.

What About a Public Relations or Marketing Plan?

Remember that customer acquisition is only part of your public relations and marketing plan. Articles in the local press spread the word but don't necessarily translate into memberships. Getting from the written word to action is much harder than other forms of marketing. You get broad exposure from local media and keep the facility's progress in the public eye, but don't depend on it for creating new customers. Local television reporters, bloggers, and print journalists are not interested in selling your project. Keep the stories you produce or offer to the journalists focused on the new facility's benefits to the community; a secondary message may mention that you are selling memberships. Radio, television, print, and billboard advertising are still effective in customer acquisition but are priced out of range for most public projects. Working out trades with radio, television, and print can be effective, but only if tracked for effectiveness. Your marketing plan continues simultaneously with your customer acquisition focus, but don't view it as the answer to turning supporters into members or finding new members.

Now is the time to call in your markers. Solicit the help of other organizations in the community that are your partners in providing service. For instance, does your facility serve as a training center for local youth swim teams? Ask them to spread the word about your facility, its positive economic impact on the community, and how it serves the general population. If scholarships are available, work with local social service organizations to get the word out that the facility is community friendly. These partners could be your best conduit to those you have not yet met or served.

Is the Plan Working?

Review your tactics or techniques to see just how effective they have been. Have the numbers in that target increased? Was it the tactic that worked, or some other unrelated variable? How should you adjust your plan? Perhaps it was the timing of the ad you placed on your local online news site. Don't be afraid to try something more than once. Learn that each failed attempt is actually a success: You now know how it won't work. Be sure to keep track of both successful and not-so-successful attempts. Over time, revisit these attempts. Perhaps they are more applicable now, or you may choose to never repeat that tactic. If you don't document it, you will not address it. Thomas Edison was once asked if he felt bad that his many attempts at the lightbulb had failed. He said that they were not failed attempts; they were purely evidence of how it would not work. That's a good attitude to adopt!

It's All About Emotions

The one thing that hasn't changed in the world of advertising and promotional campaigns is the value of human emotion. Images, humor, and heart-wrenching and inspiring messages still attract the most attention. Creating an emotional attachment to your facility is paramount in your messaging. Getting people from emotion to action is the true measure of success.

Marketing Plan

- Marketing mission
- Executive summary
- Situational analysis
- Summary of goals and objectives
  - Primary goals and objectives
  - Secondary goals and objectives
- Strategies
- Tactics
- General avenues of communication
- Emergency management information plan
- Secondary avenues of communication
- Estimated budget
- Schedule
- Tasks and assignments
- Credits

mission statement—What are you trying to accomplish?

executive summary—What are the circumstances and principal recommendations of the plan?

situational analysis—Where does your agency stand at this time regarding past memberships, major competitors, current profits, and projected financial needs?

goals and objectives—Where do you want to be, and when do you expect to get there?

strategies—What do you need to do to accomplish your objectives?

tactics—A brochure is a tactic, and so is a commercial. What will you use to meet your objectives?

general avenues of communication—What top media sources will hit your target markets?

emergency management information plan—What happens when the worst happens?

secondary avenues of communication—What is the second tier of communication to complement your plan (e.g., local free magazine listings, Parent/Teacher Organization lists)?

Consider using brief written or video testimonials from some of your early supporters. Find the most compelling reasons they supported the project, and have them make the appeal for members. Using their personal stories is much more effective than facts and figures. If those early supporters have some level of local recognition, their participation will be even more effective. Potential members will identify with them and believe them much more readily than you or your staff members.

Photos and videos of other currently operating, similar facilities can also help your sales. The general public may have to equate their experiences elsewhere, such as at a resort pool, to understand what your facility looks like. Seeing the endorsement of a resident of another community singing the praises of the zero-depth pool may just sell the concept to your customers.

Turn Supporters Into Sales Staff

Ask your early supporters to spread the word. Turn those advocates into unpaid sales personnel for the project. Ask them to network on your project's behalf and spread the word through their social media contacts, family, and friends. These are key influencers in your community. Use their power for selling your project. From Facebook to Twitter to LinkedIn, all of these sources can produce results, especially when shared within friends and family networks. Provide them with facts, figures, or photos they can upload and share in their networks.

Working with your early supporters, create a competition to bring in new members. It's a bit unorthodox in the public sector but could work. Create some freebees such as future day passes to individuals who provide new members, just like a finder's fee. Consider a special rate for those who supported the project, and get them in early. Then have them reach out to their networks and share those contacts with you.

Commit to sending out emails or, better yet, thank-you notes and coupons to the early members. These are the folks who are taking a chance that you will deliver on your promises. Handwritten notes are so rare today that you may win them over as customers for life. They will also promote you and feel bonded to you from this emotional experience. They will be amazed that you took the time to recognize their early support. These first customers are your greatest asset.

Lessons Learned

- It's not always about the project.
- Surround yourself with your enemies.
- Education is the key to valid consensus.
- Surveys without education are ineffective.
- Use community input in facility design.
- There is mistrust in local government that you must work against.
- Don't ignore the politics of the project.
- Get your face off the project and get citizens involved.
- Project supporters or those who signed petitions do not always translate into members.
- Human emotions still sell projects and products.
- Plan your techniques and tactics to fit each target market. Focus on one at a time, starting with the most profitable.
- Solicit the help of other organizations in spreading the word.
- Don't underestimate the power of the endorsement or testimonial.
- Send a thank-you note to early members or customers. They will be your most loyal supporters.

4

DESIGN TO EXCITE GUESTS

Courtesy of David Guida.

Once your aquatics project is approved, you will enter the design phase for the facility. Be sure to go back to the work you did through the public process, focus groups, and surveys, and do your best to keep your promises. While working with your architects and engineers, be sure to focus not only on the pools and attractions but also on customer service, signage, theme, accessibility, and usability. For long-term success, your design needs to be customer friendly in order to extend your guests' length of stay and to maximize your revenue. Design firms know pools, mechanical design, and chemical treatment, but not all of them know practical function and operations. You know your current customers and prospective members better than the design team does. The most beautiful designs can also be more costly in terms of supervision, maintenance, and usability.

Throughout this book, you may find the word *guests* used in two different scenarios. The first is for those public-sector operators and private swim clubs that consider a guest to be a friend of a paid member who comes along for a visit. In the resort and water-park world, everyone is considered a guest. Sure, water parks sell season passes, but they still view all who come to their property as their guests. Resorts also refer to everyone on their property as guests! It can be confusing, sure, but considering everyone as a guest is a positive approach for both public and private entities.

Parking and Entrances

From the parking lot to the bathhouse, to the snack bar, to the deck and shade, easy access for all guests should be your top priority. If guests have a bad experience in your parking lot, you've already set the stage for a questionable experience. Friendly access is key to the start of the customer experience, whether that customer is a senior citizen or a mom with a stroller. Certainly the Americans with Disabilities Act (ADA) will drive most design decisions regarding accessibility for people with challenges, but in addition, is the access friendly, manageable, and welcoming? Unless you are designing a huge facility with daily attendance in the hundreds of thousands, avoid turnstiles and other impediments for those checking into your facility. For instance, parents coming to your facility for the day may resemble mountain climbers loaded with gear—it's amazing how such small children require so much stuff!

Reception desks—or welcome centers, to use a friendlier name—should meet the requirements for the ADA and be a height that accommodates children as well. Most facilities today use a computerized swipe system with a photo ID card or a scanner. Those with larger budgets have moved on to thumb readers for admissions. All are great assets, but the most welcoming feature of any facility is a trained, friendly staff. The cleverest designs for reception desks that I have experienced are on locked castors and can be moved to accommodate staffing and crowds. After the first few seasons of a new facility, you'll have a better idea of crowd sizes and the need for fast access. On weekends, why not have a secondary gate for season-pass holders or an express lane? Having a desk on wheels can accommodate large weekend crowds in one placement and smaller, lighter crowds during the week. Some smaller facilities have found that having gate attendants sit on bar-height seats with a portable scanner is all they need at their entrances. It's a friendlier, faster, and less expensive approach.

The facilities that will benefit most from the advice in this book may not deal with any sale items at all at their entrances. Unless your facility is a tourist attraction, don't get too involved in merchandise. If you do, it may be best to sell it at your office or snack facility. One aquatic facility I worked with had a greenhouse-type window in the hallway of the bathhouse. This window served as a display for only a few items of merchandise, the kinds of products that one forgets but needs on a sunny day: disposable swim diapers, lip balm, goggles, and such. These items were on display there and could be purchased at the snack bar or manager's office.

Keep in mind the Disney approach to long lines. If you can entertain your guests while they're in line, you will make their day. On heavy attendance days, send out a gate attendant with a scanner. Ask for season-pass holders and swipe them through. My favorite signs often are best used along the admission lines. Use a sandwich board to post the prices and options. Be sure the rules are clearly posted outside the admission area so guests have time to take coolers back to the car or perhaps to dispose of any glass bottles. If you have the opportunity and space for a closed-circuit TV in your admission area, you can entertain guests with videos on behavior and drowning prevention while also telling them about prices, the weather, or the UV Index. Expecting inclement weather later in the day? Be sure to advise guests that there is a chance the facility could close early due to inclement weather.

While designing your facility with your guests in mind, remember that accidents do happen. Be sure to work with the local police, fire, and EMS to plan for transporting people in need of medical care. Be sure that there is a clear route in and out of the park in an emergency. The last thing you want is to transport victims out of your facility and wheel them right through the entry where guests are waiting to come in. This isn't good for the victim or for your facility and its reputation. You have one chance to make a good impression, and that is not the way to do it.

If you offer group sales, have another entrance plan that will not affect your season-pass holders or their guests. Bringing a large group of campers right through your admission area is a turnoff to daily guests. Use a side door or gate with a point of purchase if necessary. Be absolutely sure that you are firm on your group sales procedures, and when possible, only allow groups with reservations. Group sales should be about filling the facility when it is not otherwise busy. The walk-in or member guest experience must come first.

Guests With Unique Needs

Guests with challenges need special care and attention. Having a window at your entrance area or manager's office that says "Special Guests" can impress your guests who have unique needs. Create a brochure or short video that tells these patrons how to comfortably and safely use your facility—it's an exceptional way to win a customer forever. If necessary, have an available staff member give a tour and offer suggestions on how to best navigate the facility.

Guests with wheelchairs are often hesitant to use their chairs in and around the pool environment. Having a couple of submergible wheelchairs for free use while on your property is a wonderful customer service.

Should guests with unique needs ask for their nurse or caregiver to be admitted for free, I strongly urge you to do so. This could eliminate your obligation to provide a one-on-one lifeguard or staff member. It will also reduce any anxiety on the part of the guest or the caregiver.

Shade and Seating

Shade and seating are two of the highest-rated items in customer surveys at water parks. The days of lathering up with baby oil and iodine to bake in the sun for hours are over. Everyone knows the dangers of overexposure to the sun, and there are never enough chairs or shade at today's aquatic centers. Although grassy hills and tress are requested during design and tend to give a cool impression at a pool, guests prefer chairs, tables, and lounge chairs. If your facility can't provide these items, you may want to welcome them into the facility or perhaps even provide a storage area for the season.

Visitors gather and stake claim round umbrellas, but will line up under linear shade. It's less personal.

I've watched the behavior of guests at water parks around the world and have a whole different opinion on shade. In the 1980s and 1990s, all new outdoor pool designs included large, round umbrellas from 12 to 20 feet (4-6 m) in diameter. They give a great look to the facilities, but do they really provide enough shade? I've found that families will congregate under a round umbrella, but others are hesitant to share the shade. For new facilities, I highly recommend a combination of both round shade and linear shade. Guests are more likely to share linear shade where all those using the area are facing forward. Chaise lounges are perfect in that type of setting. This also explains why commercial parks are doing so well with cabana rentals. With stranger danger and other social ills, people want and need their privacy, especially when young children are involved.

My favorite improvement that I have urged clients to provide is a quiet zone. This is a shade pavilion that is a bit out of the way of the crowds. It can serve as a respite for a child or person with special needs who perhaps needs less stimulation, a place for a mom to breastfeed, or an area to read a book, tell a secret, or just chill out. Every facility that has followed this recommendation has received rave reviews.

I have always been a big fan of rocking chairs. As a child, I would rock in a chair to find comfort and relaxation. When the industry came out with resin rocking chairs, I jumped on the opportunity to purchase them. I saw an immediate reaction from guests, and I do believe they all became kinder and more peaceful! I have seen adults, kids, and teens rock themselves to sleep poolside. I can't keep enough of them on deck, and I can't imagine a facility without them.

Diapers, Strollers, and Babies, Oh My!

Changing tables aren't just for the women's restroom. All of the restrooms on your property should be equipped with a changing table, covered trash can, and rocking chair if available. Creating a quiet, neat, and clean environment for a nursing mom or a dad traveling with a child meets a big customer need. Providing reusable swim diapers or plastic training diapers for sale or complementary can help you avoid a code brown situation, resulting in the closing of a pool. Feces in the pool turns off customers, who in turn complain to others in the community. In the design phase, be sure to put enough family restrooms or at least restrooms with changing tables within quick reach of parents. If not, your deck and deck chairs will soon be the substitute. One day, I'm going to invent a stand-alone diaper-changing area, just like some places provide a cleaning table for fish butchering on a dock. If there are stand-alone handwashing stations at public events, why not changing tables too? Something convenient, quick, and accessible will do. It sounds crazy, I know, but if parents have to leave the pool area to change a diaper and possibly lose their chair or leave their other child unsupervised, they aren't going to go to a restroom.

Strollers can take up lots of room on pool decks and become a problem for guests who don't have children. A parking area for strollers that runs along one of your buildings and has an awning for shade can become a quiet spot for a child sleeping in a stroller or for a parent and child who need a break.

Quiet zones can make all the difference for moms and those who need a little time out.

When you design with the entire experience in mind, be sure to think like a guest. Visit other aquatic facilities. Take note of their restrooms, bathhouse, signage, shade, furnishings, and other amenities. Talk to those who are using the facility and ask what they like and dislike. Go the extra distance when thinking of guest relations. It's not only about the pools; it's about the entire experience.

One of your biggest decisions about operations will be how to determine your food service. Smaller facilities that entertain fewer than 100,000 visitors a year may only want to offer vending machines or a simple packaged-snack operation, while larger facilities may choose to find a concessionaire or operate their own food service. How does food service tie into marketing and promotions? Whatever avenue you choose for food service, be sure it is reliable, healthy, and reasonable. In terms of customer satisfaction and keeping an eye on revenue, offering a picnic area adjacent to an outdoor facility is a smart move. Customers can still visit your facility while on a budget and picnic adjacent to the property. Allowing picnic baskets in the facility will reduce per capita spending and hurt your bottom line. Offer an adjacent picnic area and you will make friends and promote multiple visits. Don't worry—there are still concession items that can't be brought in a picnic basket, like ice cream and shaved ice. Guests will still purchase those items.

Public water parks are often pressured to provide picnic areas both inside and adjacent to their facilities, but commercial properties know that in a seasonal operation, picnic baskets can ruin your revenue stream.

Whatever you choose, make sure it is done well, or you will have a public relations nightmare on your hands.

Creating Excitement for Your Project

Throughout my career I have been called a shameless self-promoter because I understood the value of branding and promotion long before many of my parks and recreation colleagues caught on. Last time I looked, there wasn't a line behind me ready to market me, my department, or my talented staff. It's up to you to create the energy! Perhaps *shameless self-promoter* should be a badge of honor, as long as it isn't at the expense of others.

I have shared various approaches to developing community consensus for an aquatic project on a budget. If you execute those steps, you've already created some buzz about your new or renovated facility. Whether that buzz is good or bad, it's still creating conversation and excitement in your community. Now you have to keep that momentum going, and it may be hard. Many public projects take years to come to fruition. A talented and committed staff will be able to continue the excitement no matter what the season or budget. It just takes some creativity, a willingness to try even if the results aren't stellar, and a sense of whimsy that will appeal to all ages. I've often referred to this approach as the *salami effect*. Am I suggesting you create a marketing and promotional plan that's like an Italian sausage? I sure am! You have to deliver excitement, one slice at a time, just like you slice salami to make a great sandwich.

As discussed earlier, there is a perception that government can never get anything done. Even though you have done a great job promoting your public meetings, referendum, study, or community consensus building, there will still be those who don't believe the facility will ever become a reality. Getting through the planning and zoning board for commercial aquatic center development is not much different—the host community must see you as an asset and not as a problem waiting to happen. It's your responsibility to find each and every opportunity to create an event, make a splash, or submit a press release to keep up the buzz.

My Least Favorite Approach

I've worked with several communities that wanted to promote their new facility and get the community excited by selling passes or memberships well in advance of the project's start or completion. Some folks in the political arena have posed this as a challenge to recreation professionals to prove there is community support. They also think that giving away memberships and passes at a promotional price will result in record numbers. This type of hype in government can easily work against you. Until people see the construction under way, they will still have the perception that this is another project the government will turn into another fine mess! If the membership sales before construction don't meet the expectations of governing bodies, panic can easily set in. In addition, projects that sell memberships with a promised opening date can find themselves in a public relations nightmare when a facility misses its projected opening day. Whether for a public or private entity, you should be prepared for possible refunds or season extensions for outdoor facilities. Think about coupons and passes for the following year that may have to be offered. Don't make promises you can't keep. It could have a two- to three-year effect on your bottom line. The public never forgets and won't be shy about reminding you of a broken promise.

My Favorites on a Budget

When I started in this business, if we were operating on a shoestring budget, all of our promotional fliers and materials were created by hand or with a stylus on mimeograph paper. Every recreation office had a mimeograph machine with a drum full of smelly ink. With advances in technology, we graduated to clip art that would be just that: clipped and pasted onto a flier and then reproduced. Those with more substantial budgets used a third-party printer, but setup, approval, printing, and distribution were time consuming and expensive. Now, more creative and affordable tools are available to all of us. There's no excuse at any budget level not to add some excitement with your promotions as you prepare for the opening of your new facility.

The most successful facilities understand the importance of making every step an event. This approach works for both public and commercial facilities. Each milestone in the project—from conceptual renderings to construction updates—should be made into an event that can attract the public's attention. Hosting a website or a page within your department's website is a great way to promote the project. With the high quality of cell-phone photography today, there's no reason not to feature photos and video of all construction milestones on your website. Communities with the good fortune of having a local or regional television station can produce construction updates on-site. There's nothing more fascinating to the public than construction, in particular specialty construction such as lazy rivers, slide towers, and slide installations. Interview the architects and engineers who are working on the project. Walk the lazy river with a group of kids and describe what the experience will be in just a few months. Take advantage of snowfall during the winter season—showing a facility in the snow can capture attention and keep the project front of mind. Cell-phone video, drone photography, and other visual construction milestones work well for all types of aquatic facility development. Cell phones make all of these things attainable and affordable no matter what your budget.

While working on the Crystal Springs Family Waterpark, city websites didn't exist, but our local-access TV was the outlet for video production. During the winter months, I dressed in snow gear, laid on a chaise lounge at the construction site singing "Let It Snow," and then pitched an early membership rate. I sat in a snow-covered slide and dangled my feet into a pool full of snow to pitch job opportunities. Sure, the commercials didn't win any critical media awards, but they did get the attention of residents and recognition from the World Waterpark Association (WWA) for the grassroots effort.

Consider holding a Show Us Your Snowman contest and offer a free membership to the best snowman photo sent to your Facebook page while your facility is under construction. Challenge participants to dress the snowman in bathing suits, goggles, and life vests. People love to show off their artistic abilities, and winning a membership is fabulous. A simple contest can turn into a promotion for the new facility.

Smartphones now offer easy access to video production. Free apps that allow for time-lapse photography and other video effects are readily available. Working with local college or high school students can really pay off because they know what attracts teens and millennials.

Drone photography is also readily available. From amateur to commercial quality, drone aerial photography is a great way to get your message out. People are fascinated by the drone's-eye view and will be drawn to your website or local TV station to see more. Three-dimensional imagery is also now available at reasonable costs and will allow residents to take a virtual tour of the facility before construction begins.

Be sure to call attention to the new facility's location with a "Coming Soon" sign themed to match the facility. This can be done with a traditional plywood sign or a huge banner. Vinyl banners have also improved in quality, and the prices are more reasonable than ever. Post signs or banners on the side of the building to be constructed or at the park that will host the new aquatic center. Using an inexpensive sign material like Coroplast, put several four-by-four-foot (122 × 122 cm) concept renderings and floor plans at large public gathering spaces, such as the library, senior center, and city hall, for maximum exposure. When ready to unveil the new sign or banner, make a celebration out of it. Cover it with tarps, invite the press, ship in some kids with tubes and goggles, and unveil the sign at a press conference. Now that's an event!

My friends at Tropicanoe Cove in Indiana came up with an ambitious and creative approach that I still marvel at today. At the site of their new facility, they painted the footprint of some of the attractions. They put lifeguard chairs along the painted lazy river, had staff pose as lifeguards, scattered tubes along the river, and invited kids to come and swim (i.e., walk) the river. The kids got hard hats and other promotional items while they walked through the painted plans. That's not an event; that's an experience. All of these efforts paved the way for huge crowds and lots of early memberships.

Facility trivia is a good way to get the attention of those fascinated with facts. Why not hold a contest to guess how many gallons of water the pool holds? Or how many concrete trucks it takes to build a lazy river? Factoids help create a vision for the public and can keep the interest alive.

You Gotta Have a Gimmick

In the musical *Gypsy*, there's a song featuring an exotic dancer who plays the trumpet. Her signature song is "You Gotta Have a Gimmick." Being a huge Broadway fan, I've always remembered that song and message. What's your gimmick that will make your new facility stand out from all other leisure options? What do you want folks to think about when deciding where to spend their time and money? In East Brunswick, New Jersey, Crystal Springs was all about sparkling-clean water after years of swimming in a brackish pond. Whenever possible, crystals were used in advertising and promotions. Crystals in beautifully wrapped boxes were gifts to all the VIPs. Crystal-clear water was emphasized, and crystals were given out at township events, farmers markets, and other locations where they could deliver their message. Sparkles and crystals can be purchased quite inexpensively online and in local craft stores. Craft tables for kids at events sponsored by the city can have coloring contests, crafts with crystals, and more. It's all up to you, your imagination, and the willingness of your staff to take a chance.

Ribbon-Cutting Ceremonies

It's a tradition in most American cities to have both a planned groundbreaking ceremony and a ribbon-cutting ceremony. The tradition involves the participants wearing hard hats and digging up dirt with a ceremonial shovel. That's certainly a good press opportunity, as well as a politically correct move, but what more can you make out of the event? How about asking participants in the ceremony wear safari helmets or baseball caps with your logo? Ask hosts in Hawaiian shirts to walk participants around the property, explaining the features of the new equipment. Be sure to have a professional-quality press packet and a press table for everyone to check in at. Provide each member of the press with an ambassador to answer questions and introduce the important players. Offer a food cart previewing the types of snack foods you expect to serve. Play a 3D video walk-through and promotional pieces on video monitors during the food-and-drink portion of the event. Dress the area with colorful banners that reflect your theme. If your mascot is in place, it must be present. Keep the press representatives well fed and entertained, provide them with a souvenir, and give them quality facts that will be interesting to their readers.

When possible, schedule the ribbon-cutting ceremony as a soft opening of the new aquatic center. Do the ceremonial ribbon-cutting photo op, and then invite a local youth organization to come use the park following the ribbon cutting. Keep the invites to those who supported the project or were instrumental in its evolution. This way, it serves as a political necessity as well as an opportunity for your staff to work out the kinks in all the systems before trying to host a record crowd.

Have a grand opening celebration on your true opening day that involves entertainment such as music, live entertainers, and contests. If you've done your preopening promotions well, your new aquatic center will be packed with guests who are not the slightest bit interested in speeches or presentations. You will have lots more to think about than just the opening ceremony. You may want to focus on the first kid down the slide, or have the mayor ride the slide in a tuxedo. Select someone truly special to ride the first slide, such as a local war hero, first responder, contest winner, or other significant community leader. Or, you could work with a community nonprofit organization to auction off the first ride down the slide for charity. This can offer lots of cross promotion and some good karma too. Create an opening-day photo op that will be easily captured for press use. Be sure it makes a great splash!

It only takes time and imagination to make every step in your facility's evolution an event. Make it an event or experience, and the excitement will fill the facility for years to come.

Lessons Learned

- There is never enough shade.
- Diaper-changing tables need to be close to the pools and in all restrooms.
- There are never enough chairs.
- Swift admissions and friendly signage and service begin the guest experience.

- Make a good impression from the start, and you'll enhance the guest experience.
- Everything and every event matters in preopening promotions.
- You need a gimmick. Get that theme early and use it always.
- Treat the press well; your success is in their hands.
- Give the public a slice at a time, like a good salami sandwich.
- Build the excitement piece by piece; it's a slow burn, not a bonfire.

5

APPEAL TO SPECIFIC POPULATIONS

Aquatics means different things to different generations and people in different stages of life. Learning what makes each specific population want to support your facility will help you effectively market to that population, ensure that the facility design meets the needs of your major targets, and increase your bottom line. This chapter focuses on marketing to several unique populations: moms, tweens, empty nesters, and baby boomers.

Winning Over the Mommy Market

Faith Popcorn and Lys Marigold's hit book *Eveolution* was just the start of the examination of the differences between the female consumer and her male counterpart. In the aquatic industry, both male and female adults of all ages become members of our facilities with fitness and relaxation in mind. It is when these singles become parents that their interests and priorities change in many ways, including their expectations for service, cleanliness, and safety. When female consumers become members of the so-called mommy market, they become some of the most outspoken, engaged, and critical recipients of the services we offer.

In *Eveolution* (Popcorn and Marigold 2000) , the facts are clear: Women buy or influence the purchase of 80 percent of all consumer goods. They make 80 percent of all leisure purchase decisions for their families. They purchase 51 percent of consumer electronics, influence 80 percent of all health care decisions, and buy 50 percent of all cars and influence 80 percent of their sales. In addition, women make up 48 percent of all stock market investors and outearn their husbands in 22.7 percent of American households. They also head 40 percent of households with assets over $600,000.

These statistics scream, "You've come a long way, baby!" They are important to just about every consumer industry, especially the leisure and travel industries. Still not a believer? Why are websites for home food delivery multiplying by the day? Why are spas and other pampering products now purchased at higher rates than ever? Online retailers understand that women tend to be emotional buyers and enjoy the hunt, while men purchase based on other factors (Brennan 2009).

In our industry, we've long known that most of the aquatic decisions are made by the female head of the household, but do we understand why she buys and what keeps her coming back to our facilities? Before we can understand what motivates the female customer, we have to watch the trends nationally, do our best to understand those market drivers, and apply them to our facilities.

You don't have to have studied marketing to become a trend spotter. I've watched how many industries have grown through the support of female consumers. Web purchases, parties for selling home and beauty products, high-end industrial kitchen appliances, organic and diet food delivery, the NFL (National Football League) line of sportswear for women, and how a simple mention of a product by a respected female star turns it into a gold mine are key clues to what women want. The challenge is to apply this information to what we do to capture the attention of the female head of the household and keep her coming back.

Women tend to be brand loyal. As a child and then a teen, I used the beauty products my mom and sisters used. To this day, I'm still loyal to the family brand of both shampoo and perfume. Now, that's loyalty—and I am not an anomaly. Understanding our female customers and what pleases them is the secret to keeping the mommy market happy when they visit our facilities.

Men and women differ in so many ways, but scientists throughout history have known that women and men perceive thoughts, colors, smells, textures, voices, and sounds differently. A perfect example of this is the difference in reactions between men and women using bathhouses. You just finished power washing both the men's and women's restrooms shortly before opening for the day. Men perceive the water on the floor as just that: water. Women, however, perceive it as messy, sloppy, and perhaps some type of bodily fluid! I've witnessed this many times throughout my career. It's all about perceptions, expectations, and priorities.

Cater to those who make most of the leisure decisions.

In the report *Destination Marketing 101: Take Care of Mom*, the author John R. Hendrie, the CEO of Hospitality Performance, Inc., states that the top priorities in selling leisure products to moms are cleanliness, safety and security, physical conditions, and service. This is the formula for success in managing aquatic facilities. The other bells and whistles of our programs and special events matter, but those basics are the deal-makers and breakers when it comes to water parks and aquatic centers.

Creating a Female-Friendly Facility

Now that you know the top priorities in selling leisure products to moms, how do you apply this to your operations? Although safety has to be the highest priority, the female guest will pay special attention to the restrooms, bathhouse, and physical environment. Women tend to notice and react to peeling paint or wet floors much sooner than men. With health, wellness, and safety in mind, consider programming directed toward your female guests, such as fitness, yoga, paddleboarding, ladies nights, and spa-like environments. The female consumer is service focused. Examine the services you provide and tailor them to the female consumers who make the majority of leisure and travel decisions.

The mommy market also needs some special considerations such as stroller parking, convenient and clean restrooms, and lots of shade. In general, once a woman claims her space—whether it be a chair, chaise lounge, or shade structure—she will remain and often will not welcome others in. Remember that privacy and security rank high for the female consumer. With stranger danger in the news every day, all parents are protective, but don't dare cross the mama bear. I know that men now reading this book may call me sexist and tell me they have the same concerns. I'm female and I understand these decision drivers. I respect my male guests and also cater to their needs, but in the family market, a family-friendly environment is paramount to the female decision maker.

Creating a Family-Friendly Environment

From the bathhouse to the snack bar, there are special considerations to create a family-friendly environment. Young families in particular may need special hours to accommodate nap time. A 12 o'clock opening of an outdoor family aquatic center is already close to lunch and nap time, meaning that young children may not get to use the facility as much as their older siblings.

Shade is so important to a family-friendly environment. When possible, provide grassy spaces or picnic tables under trees to create a quiet zone for guests who need to nap. These kinds of spaces can also become entertainment areas for a children's entertainer or musician.

Providing special events and activities for the youngest guests is particularly appealing to young families. Working with your local library or bookstore, why not have story times? Appoint a staff member to run games and activities for kids of all ages, including the smallest of your guests.

Should you choose to sell merchandise or give it away for promotions, include items such as bibs, hats, and T-shirts for the little ones. These can be coveted items by parents and will be adorable marketing tools when worn around the community.

Playgrounds are often part of a municipal water park, but special considerations should be made to ensure the equipment doesn't grow too hot for bare legs and feet. Child-sized picnic tables or Adirondack chairs make kids feel grown up and just like their siblings. Parents love them, too. My favorite kid-centric amenity is a sandbox with dinosaur bones cemented into the base. Every day, aspiring paleontologists dig to find the dinosaur and can start all over again the next day. It may not be the favorite of your maintenance staff, but kids love it.

For many young guests, their time at the community pool can become quite long, especially on cloudy days. Having other entertainment opportunities is attractive to families. Create a lending library where guests of all ages can take or bring a book. Magazines and puzzle books are also popular. Your community library may be willing to give you their cast-offs.

Don't underestimate the value of games such as table tennis, Nok Hockey, and four square. Create spaces where these activities can take place, and make board games available. It's a simple service but one that increases the perceived value of your membership. You'll make the dreaded rain delay more manageable by having a fun box with books, toys, puzzles, chalk, and coloring books that kids can use while hunkered down in the bathhouse waiting for the rain to pass. Playing children's songs during the rain delay, including "Rain, Rain, Go Away," is a fun ritual that they will come to look forward to.

Happy babies, happy mommy, happy everyone.

In earlier chapters, I've shared insights into making your facility comfortable and accessible to all. Parents are often carrying lots of stuff: diaper bags, strollers, toys, lunch boxes, and more. Make their arrival easy and convenient by ensuring that entrances are wide enough to allow families to enter without getting hung up on gates or turnstiles. Sell items such as swim diapers and sunblock at the front desk so parents can survive the day if they forget something.

Evening activities that cater to couples with children are also popular and are a great way for new residents to meet others with similar interests. Date nights at aquatic venues with babysitting available give parents the opportunity to enjoy the facility as well. When visiting Sweden, a mecca for year-round community aquatic facilities, date nights complete with tablecloths and candles on picnic tables are common and well received. Taking care of Mom's and Dad's needs is important in family-driven facilities too.

Should You Sell to Tweens?

Before you can successfully sell to any target market, you must understand how that group lives, thinks, behaves, and buys. Selling to kids, in particular to tweens, can increase your bottom line and fill your aquatic center. Once kids are old enough to visit our facilities alone, they become a separate target market. Kids aged 8 to 14 are known as being in the age of compression. They are extremely different from the last generation of kids. They grow up faster and are more connected, direct, and informed.

Parental Responsibility Campaigns

Parents need to know and understand their responsibilities when they are poolside with their children. Parents of young children are always interested in safety. Posting safety rules and parental responsibility information in areas where young families congregate is vital to educating parents. Quick poolside demonstrations in the use of an AED and advice on how to purchase a life vest for personal use are well received. Reinforcing these responsibilities will be valued by the parents and may save a life.

Recruiting community volunteers to serve as deck ambassadors at your facility is a great use of committed volunteers. Retirees are naturals for this type of volunteer service. For example, have them circulate among guests, do diaper inspections, provide approved diapers, and explain why the diapers are needed. Deck ambassadors can also circulate information on drowning prevention and other safety issues.

Free Wi-Fi at facilities is pretty much the standard today, but do we really want parents on their phones and not watching their children? In Australia, some municipal facilities provide a message when guests sign on to their free Wi-Fi. The message is a child with a small sign saying, "You should be watching me, not your phone." The campaign is brilliant and to the point.

They have more power, money, influence, and attention than generations of kids before them. They have financial savvy and, of course, they are wired electronically.

Why Sell to Tweens?

Today's generation of tweens spends $150 billion a year in the United States alone. They spend $1 trillion globally and influence their parents to spend another $150 billion per year.

Tweens influence their parents' purchases of major items such as cars, phones, clothes, and homes. You just have to watch prime-time television commercials to notice that car sales, high-end watches, and electronics are targeted to kids because they are key influencers in these types of prestige purchases. Kids make many purchase requests daily, whether out shopping, at home, or on vacation. According to Dr. James U. McNeal, author of *The Kids Market* (1999), statistics show that kids are now influencing the choice of vacation destinations and high-end accommodations. It feels foreign to me as a child of the 1950s who would never have had the slightest influence on how my parents spent money. We didn't have any to spend, but I'm sure they wouldn't have consulted me!

With tweens, they are all about the brand. They turn to brand names for security. They may be quick to brand an aquatic facility as boring, benign, and outdated. Tweens buy brands and then influence their parents to do the same. They grow into and out of brands quickly. You had better hope they haven't negatively branded your facility, because it will be hard to undo.

How Are Tweens Different?

Studies have shown that tweens now have less imagination and creativity than previous generations (McNeal 1999). They demand instant gratification and have a tendency to be insecure and depressed. Tweens are highly motivated by fear and are often agitated by fear-based marketing. This generation often has trouble with verbal communication and face-to-face confrontation. Perhaps because of their growing dependence on cell phones and social media, their interpersonal skills can be weak. They think interactively and in full color. They have an interest in money, and many in the United States have their own bank accounts. Kids are bombarded by thousands of brands per day in commercials and product placement in movies, TV shows, and video games. Knowing this information can help you to better understand tweens as customers and influence their purchases; in turn, they can influence their parents' choices. In Martin Lindstrom and Patricia Seybold's 2004 book *Brand Child*, the authors explain the six core values in marketing to tweens:

1. Stability
2. Humor
3. Fear
4. Mastery
5. Fantasy
6. Love

Recognizing these motivators in this age group will help you be successful in programming and marketing to them. Some ideas might include special events that involve themes of mystery and fantasy, or collecting pins, buttons, and other incentives. Humor, especially at the expense of adults, is especially attractive to this group. An adult belly-flop contest will be all the rage with tweens. Kids love to see adults vulnerable and looking silly. Watch a few sitcoms on the Disney Channel, and you'll see that kids love to poke fun at their parents. *Harry Potter*, *Shrek*, and other movies and books have been wildly successful by using all of these prime motivators of kids and tweens.

Teens and tweens can be hard to please. Just ask them what they want.

Here are questions to ask yourself and your staff when punching up the volume on your tween marketing:

- To what degree is your agency dependent on tweens? Establish that value, and budget for it.
- If you don't currently attract the tween market, what can you do to encourage them to choose your facility?
- Has your aquatic center been branded by tweens? Is the brand good, bad, or nonexistent? You will need to turn that around using the six core values.
- Are tweens proud to wear your brand?
- Do you use social media for tween interaction?
- Are tweens attracted enough to your brand to influence their parents and act as references for your aquatic center and its programming?

Empty Nesters Have Full Pockets

Empty-nest syndrome is the depression and loneliness some parents feel when one or more of their children leave home. It is much more common in women, but it can happen to both sexes. The marriage of a child, although usually a joyous event, can also kick this syndrome into gear.

What is the prescribed treatment for folks suffering from this syndrome? It is advised that they find new activities and distractions to take up some of their time. Empty nesters who successfully survive this syndrome have plans in place for their extra time, money, and space. It seems like this would be a time to celebrate, but change is hard at any age, especially for this generation of parents.

With rising housing and health care costs, lots of empty nesters need not worry about being left alone because their kids might just come back, at least for a while. An increasing number of adult children between the ages of 25 and 34 are now living at home. These boomerang kids return due to economics, divorce, extended education, drug or alcohol problems, or temporary transitions.

As you plan your aquatic center and develop your admission prices and membership fees, you may find two generations in the same household that often get overlooked in public-sector programs and activities. Even the commercial water-park industry has only just begun to focus on empty nesters and their single, childless adult children.

Who Are the Baby Boomers?

People born after World War II (around 1943) and before the Vietnam War (around 1963) can be considered baby boomers. Most baby boomers now are empty nesters; the generation after them has moved on to their own lives. Baby boomers have the highest median incomes in the United States. They tend to reevaluate their lives in middle age, formerly known as the midlife crisis. They have a tendency to micromanage and prefer religion over science. They support tough-love approaches toward addicts and criminal offenders, and they tend to come out to vote. Boomers have a passion for personal and social improvement now that they have more free time without the constant caregiving needed by a family at home. They have a tendency to be a bit ageist, and they don't want to be viewed as seniors.

The more you understand the character traits of boomers, the more you will understand that they are an excellent target market for aquatic venues. What else makes them tick?

They are better educated and more optimistic than their parents. They are comfortable with technology, although many were late to today's technology. Most are self-taught in all things electronic but are open to experimenting and focused on convenience. Boomers are individualistic and self-focused, and they tend to reject authority. That's the former hippie in many of them! They strive to control the aging process and now have time to focus on themselves. They are spenders rather than savers and are comfortable with credit. They may joke about spending their children's inheritance, but they mean it!

Their focus on controlling the aging process makes baby boomers willing to pay for health and beauty aids, dietary supplements, and prescription drugs; thus, it may seem there is a pharmacy on every block. This generation is open to plastic surgery to keep aging at bay. They are readers, and they love gadgets. The minivan gets traded in for the latest luxury car. They typically spend on quality garments and name brands. This generation sees the years ahead and wants to make the most of them.

Boomers are politically involved and aware. They are concerned about the environment for their children's and grandchildren's future. There are about 78 million boomers, and they have expendable income.

This generation grooved to Led Zeppelin, Madonna, the Red Hot Chili Peppers, and Kiss. They were influenced by *Doonesbury*, *Forrest Gump*, *American Pie*, Steve Jobs, *The Color Purple*, and *Saturday Night Live*. Half of all boomers are over the age of 50, and every day another 10,000 join them. They have tremendous buying power. No wonder Disney has had them as their target-market focus for the past decade and caters to all of their interests.

So what are the implications for your aquatic center? If your marketing plan still only targets 18- to 49-year-olds, you are missing millions of potential customers who are over 50 and looking for what aquatic facilities can offer them.

Will Boomers Increase Your Bottom Line?

Let's discuss how boomers can increase your bottom line. When you win over members of this generation, they will be loyal and politically supportive. Catering to their needs means they will not only make your cash register ring, but they will also support your funding, expansion, and services.

Besides political power, they have economic power. According to an article on BabyBoomer-Magazine.com by Daryl Burns (2011), 70 percent of the nation's net worth is in American baby boomers' hands. They have more discretionary income than any other age group, own 80 percent of all money in savings and loan institutions for a total of $7 trillion in wealth, and are fanatically loyal to brands. They will spend nearly $40 million in the next year, and that's only on their children.

Since the early 2000s, boomers without kids have increased their food and beverage spending at twice the rate of other age groups. Most boomers work in some capacity and are open to volunteer experiences. Not only will they be consumers of your programs, but they just might work or volunteer for you.

How Do You Sell to Boomers?

Marketing teams must make sure that what the aquatic facility offers is perceived as a good value for the money. Your programs and products need to have wide appeal to meet varied needs. If boomers are not happy, they will switch to the next facility up the road. Back in the day they didn't trust anyone over 30; now they don't trust anyone under 30!

When reaching your boomer targets through advertising, social media, or the electronic press, be sure to talk with the boomers, not at them. Sell experience, not age. Ditch the senior adult mantle, or they won't buy it! *Active adults* seem to be the new buzz words in the industry. Use the words *mature*, *prime*, or *vital* in your ads. Inspire them to buy by focusing on fun, fitness, and vitality. When choosing photos, use age-appropriate, healthy, active role models to attract their interest. The images need to be attainable for them; otherwise, they will turn them off. Be sure to select larger font sizes and simple styles with subtle color combinations. Boomers love to reminisce about "back in the day," and they relate to the candy, cartoons, TV shows, songs, and fashion of their generation.

Courtesy of Gretchen Masterfano.

80 is the new 60. Seniors are now active adults!

What Should Employees Know About Boomers and Empty Nesters?

Good customer service is important to all of your guests. It has been my experience that customer service is a marketing tool as important as any print, electronic, or social media, especially to this generation. Employees need to know the following:

- Staff will spend more time with this segment than any other.
- They welcome personal relationships with your staff; they want you to recognize and appreciate their support of your facility.
- This generation wants and deserves respect. Call them *Mr.* or *Mrs.* Don't use first names with guests from this group until they invite it.
- Speak directly; eye contact and a good handshake are significant to them.
- Use promotions that speak to distinctions in lifestyle, stage in life, and health concerns.
- Create rituals, and market with feelings and emotions.
- They have many layers and needs to be met.
- Appeal to their interests and generational markers.
- They make loyal and punctual employees, especially in retirement jobs.
- Go to them and prove yourself. Use coupons and special promotions.

How Do You Keep Them Coming Back?

Boomers will leave you if you don't address their needs. They will go elsewhere, because they are mobile. Not addressing their unique needs is foolish and can hurt the financial future of your agency. As American cities age, so do their residents. Many communities are finding that the percentage of boomers is quickly outpacing young families.

Boomers and empty nesters can bring other new customers to you as well, such as their grandchildren. Grandparents are taking on child care for their grandchildren at high rates now that two working parents are the American norm.

Catering to both empty nesters and baby boomers will result in a positive impact on your revenue. Flexible schedules and one-on-one fitness classes fit their lifestyles. The generation before them sat in senior centers all day long for socialization and recreation. Boomers, on the other hand, are on the go. They will come for a lap swim or aquacize and then head off to their busy lives. You will start to change the way you do business as your area or region ages.

Water-park and aquatic center design in the past focused only on thrill rides, water cannons, and the kid and teen market. Finding a balance in programming and design will draw this generation to those attractions. Walking against the current of a lazy river for exercise is an example of making one attraction fit all.

I recognized the differences in generations when I thought about my dad. His generation had two pairs of shoes: work shoes and funeral shoes. Look into the closet of a man in his 60s today and you may see shoes for boating, bowling, hiking, skiing, golf, tennis, and running.

Although there are plenty of ways to incorporate boomers into your programming and special events, you can also provide activities and events just for this generation. Poolside dinners, adult-only swims, ladies' nights, and couples' swims can encourage those without children to consider your facility when choosing where to spend their leisure time.

When I first saw Disney's ads and promotions for couples whose children have grown up, I thought they were insane. But boy, did they get it right. They focused on that quest for nostalgia and desire for adult indulgences like nightclubs, spas, golf, and high-end accommodations. When you see success like Disney's, adapt it to your facility. Mix in education on fitness, weight maintenance, spirituality, and mindfulness, and you have a winning combination for this generation.

Still not convinced this will work? Take a look at Disney's stats on adults without children who visit Disney World, as reported by Lauren Lipton (2013):

- Each year 51 million people visit Walt Disney World.
- About one-third of those are adults without children.
- Adult admissions at amusement parks are up around the country.

Additionally, Disney World is one of the world's largest purveyors of fine wines (Disney 2007).

My best advice to those trying to improve their marketing to a specific target market is to become a great observer of trends in marketing, advertising, and product design. If you become a student of all the messages delivered through TV, movies, radio, and social media, you can mimic the best of those campaigns and integrate them into your own marketing. Bring together people from the age group you need to target, and ask them what they need and what motivates them. Listen more than you talk. Hear them and respect their input. They will help you define your goals.

Lessons Learned

- The female head of the household makes the majority of the leisure decisions for families.
- Female consumers are extremely loyal once you've won them over.
- Cleanliness is just as important as safety to the female consumer.
- Convenience and access are crucial to young families.
- The perception of cleanliness differs between male and female guests.
- Kids can be influential. Sell to kids and their parents will follow.
- Tweens are brand sensitive. If your aquatic center has been branded as lame, you have lots of work to do to win them back.
- Kids have disposable income. Apply the six core values to what you do.
- Keep your promises to tweens. They not only influence other age groups, but they also influence their peers.
- Special events and programming based on the six core values will punch up the volume and make your events and programs attractive to this group.
- Empty nesters and baby boomers may need more attention, but they are loyal members and advocates.
- Providing opportunities for fitness and wellness on a flexible schedule will make your programming successful for this age group.
- Boomers are sensitive to labels such as *senior*.
- Active adults are the fastest-growing segment in society. Aquatic centers have to be ready to meet their needs.
- Baby boomers are likely to spend their money on all things fitness and health when the perceived value is good and the programs are high quality.

6

PRICE SMARTLY

So many factors are involved with marketing an aquatic center that you may think that pricing, membership categories, and admission policies are the least of your problems. But I hope to change your thinking as we explore the impact of pricing and its relationship to the perceived value of your facility. Before you price your new or improved facility, understand that unless you are in a tourist market, raising prices will be a challenge. Make sure to start at the pricing level that is best for your market and your financial goals. Think how much easier pricing must be for those in resort areas where a new group of tourists arrives every week. Except for the cost of changing your signs, you could adjust fees pretty easily without the previous visitors ever finding out!

Regional and community facilities don't have the luxury of new guests every week, so pricing must be balanced and fair. The best money spent in the planning stages of any new or expanded facility is on the financial feasibility study. You can hire a firm to conduct such a study at reasonable rates, considering the expense of a new facility. In fact, a financial feasibility study is imperative before you even venture into an expansion or new facility.

Most financial feasibility studies consist of two main components: a market study and a financial analysis. They take into consideration the local demographics and identify the potential success of your facility within the service area. This helps identify what type of facility will have the greatest success. They also help you to determine the mix of features that will best fit your budget and revenue picture. They then look at the cost of construction and operations, and translate those into valuable information for the design team and the owner-operator. Whether you commission a study or attempt it in-house, you need to look beyond a local user survey or emotional appeal from residents. Those are great motivators but don't realistically reflect the market. Consider things such as the site, accessibility of utilities, neighboring uses, proximity to transportation, and area demographics. Do you intend to reach only your community, or will you be reaching out in a 20- to 25-mile (32-40 km) radius? Is there competition for the leisure dollar? Are similar facilities available? Should you duplicate or supplement the services provided by others? The weather conditions, length of the season, availability of affordable employees and lifeguards, and estimated attendance numbers should all be analyzed as a part of good financial planning.

After evaluating the market feasibility of the facility, the financial analysis then looks deeply into the overall finances of the facility, including operating expenses, capital debt, and net operating income. When planning a public facility, what is the desired financial outcome? The term *per cap* includes the overall spending at your facility per person per day. This includes projections for what a visitor will spend on admission, food concessions, and other items such as tube rentals and merchandise.

You will start to see that the cost of admission or membership to your aquatic center can influence what customers will spend on other items, including upgrading for special conditions or premiums. If admission is priced too high for your area, the per cap will likely go down for items such as the snack bar and merchandise. Finding the right balance is a job for a seasoned professional who specializes in the finances of your type of project.

What Is Entertainment Value?

The phrase *entertainment value* is well understood in the private waterpark community. It may be new, though, to public aquatic operators and commercial fitness facilities. Entertainment value relates to the amenities offered by your new or expanded aquatic center. The level of entertainment determines how long a guest will stay in your facility. When the entertainment value is high, the length of stay increases and in turn so does the per cap. Aquatic facilities of all types, even those built for the Olympic Games, now reflect the importance of entertainment value for financial viability. The 1950s idea of the successful aquatic facility as a rectangular hole in the ground filled with crisp blue water is long gone. Entire generations have now grown up with the concept that pools are not just for swim lessons, competitive and fitness swimming, and the occasional game of Marco Polo. Even small fitness facilities and college campuses have come to understand that guests expect some entertainment. Facilities that combine fitness swimming, competitive training, and swim lessons with family leisure pools, zero-depth entries, slides, and attractions have the greatest potential for long-term success.

Luckily, there are plenty of inexpensive options for creating or improving entertainment value that are addressed in other chapters. Here, we will focus on pricing strategies that take into account all that your facility has to offer.

Finding the Balance in Admission Pricing

There are as many strategies for pricing as there are patterns for bathing suits. You have to find the pricing strategy that fits your demographic and helps achieve the results outlined in your financial planning. Keep in mind that some of the following concepts for creating your pricing structure can also increase and maintain your membership.

One strategy that does not work is setting low prices so more people will come. Don't underestimate your value; a very low price point screams lack of entertainment value. In the public sector, this often happens as a result of emotional and political decisions. "What about the low-income kids?" is often the platform for debate about pricing in public aquatic centers. For both public and private aquatic centers, there are fabulous ways to accommodate those families most in need without giving away the facility with a low admission price. I'll share those strategies with you in a later chapter.

Remember that it is always easier to offer special pricing, sales, coupons, early-bird memberships, and other promotions to lower the admission fee. It's much more difficult to raise a fee. This is especially hard in the public sector, where prices are often set by ordinance. And if you raise fees often, you may create a marketing challenge while sending mixed signals to guests about the value of your facility.

Different regions of the country and different types of aquatic facilities create structures that are familiar to their potential guests. In the

What's It Cost to Catch a Flick?

The average length of stay at an outdoor aquatic facility with a good entertainment value is usually about four hours. If it costs $10 to see a movie that provides two hours of entertainment, you could use that as the basis for your daily rate. A daily rate for a small to midsized water park could command $20 per day for an adult, and less for a child or senior. Equate your aquatic experience to other leisure pursuits in your region to create your pricing strategy, keeping in mind your demographics.

Midwest, for example, most public facilities offer a daily guest rate as well as a season pass. In the Northeast, seasonal and annual memberships seem to be the norm, with daily guests being accompanied by members and no walk-in guests. Because of the wide variety of facilities and pricing strategies, you may need to modify the admission concepts found in this chapter and decide how best to present them to your potential guests or members.

Does One Price Fit All?

The simplest approach is one price admits all. This approach takes the position that everyone who enters your facility needs to be attended to, regardless of age. The American public, however, has gotten used to the idea that kids and seniors should pay less. In public facilities, senior pricing is almost always done because of the vocal senior population; oftentimes, it's a necessity to get a referendum passed for a new aquatic center. The concept of seniors and children paying less for admission to a public or commercial facility is the opposite of their use patterns. They have the most free time and spend the most time at your property, yet they are often the guests who require the most attention for medical issues and behavior. I've been watching other industries raise the age of a senior pass and lower the age of a child's pass. The ski industry in the Rockies used to provide a discounted or free ski pass for seniors over 70. As seniors are now labeled *active adults*, the age of senior free or reduced passes has climbed. One day, all guests should pay the same for a visit to a facility regardless of age because they all require supervision. The political reality is that it will never happen.

How about a family rate? This is often the most debated admission rate because it requires you to define *family*. In our ever-evolving society, that isn't always easy. For marketing and public relations credibility, be careful with this definition. When considering a family rate, I have found it best to define *family* as immediate family and accept up to two adults and all dependent children under the age of 18 years. You'll often hear the question "My husband doesn't come to the water park, so why should he pay?" when someone is considering a season pass. This is yet another great argument for charging one price for all admissions. Keep the family rate simple because you will often get much debate, such as "They have five kids and I only have three!" I've seen facilities bend to this type of debate and create an admissions structure that is longer than the menu at a Jersey diner. Keep your pricing strategy as simple and innocuous as possible.

Another potential stumbling block in pricing is the age of a child for admission. In most facilities, once children reach the age of two, they are considered members at the child or individual rate; children under two are typically admitted free of charge with a parent. Although a child of two could never attend a facility alone, it creates a starting point for your other pricing. At what age should children be allowed to visit an aquatic center alone or have their own membership? Age 11 or 12 is often when children are considered to be independent enough to come to your center alone.

Courtesy of Gretchen Masterfano.

Under 2 goes free. Most facilities start charging at 2 years of age.

Allow All Children to Participate

The age of a swimmer, as well as ability to swim, has become a great debate in urban aquatic centers. Understanding that the cost of swimming lessons and their availability in cities has caused a gap in the swimming ability of minority youth, we have to carefully set our policies. The rules of the 1960s stated that children under a certain age or those who could not swim were not allowed to visit a public or private pool unless accompanied by a parent. That rule was common in neighborhoods where at least one parent was home and available. But the concern about unattended youth in city pools has caused a steep decline in use, resulting in some pools falling into disrepair because their attendance numbers don't justify investing money into the facility. The concern over swimmer safety can be overcome with the use of swim testing, life vests, and learn-to-swim programs. The bottom line is this: When creating admission and pricing policies, don't eliminate the aquatic experience for children who can benefit from and enjoy it.

Season Passes

Season passes to an aquatic center are a great idea for creating early cash flow. But, these season passes have to be carefully priced and timed to make financial sense for your facility. Season-pass rates are determined by the average number of visits for a season. Most outdoor facilities have an 80- to 100-day season. Multiple the daily rate by 8 to 10 visits, and you have the basis of your season-pass fee. Customers feel they are getting a good deal, and you can initiate marketing buzz with the season-pass promotions. Beware, though, that the season-pass holder isn't your biggest overall spender and is often the hardest to please. Except for the major amusement parks, season-pass holders pack their own lunches, don't visit the merchandise shop often, and complain the most. Set the timing for your season-pass sales to end by the end of the school year or by July 4 at the latest. No matter what your geographical location or weather patterns, outdoor swimming patterns are pretty consistent. Once the fall sport season arrives, attendance drops even in warm climates. Spring and fall are shoulder seasons as far as attendance goes, even in states with generally warm climates. This is a weather-related business, and folks will wait it out to see how the weather will be.

You might also consider offering a half-price season in the second half of the season. If August sees decreased attendance for your outdoor

Everybody gets into the act when fantasy abounds.

facility or the winter season slows for your indoor facility, discount during those times. Keep careful watch on attendance numbers and patterns at your facility, and only discount the times that are least used. Bundling or packaging tickets or memberships to a variety of facilities owned and operated by the same entity does have customer appeal, but I caution you to approach this concept carefully after a thorough examination of use patterns. Offering too many discounts or packages can become confusing and lower the perceived value of the facilities in the bundle. Always think of bundling facilities that lack high attendance. Use this strategy as a draw to facilities with marginal attendance, and don't give away your premium properties.

Tickets for Trade

One of the best tools for marketing your aquatic center is to trade with other companies and agencies that can maximize your exposure and improve your bottom line. Trading tickets for radio and television ads is an easy way to market your facility. Trading for other products or merchandise that you need in exchange for tickets can also work; just be sure your staff members understand that the tickets aren't free. Tickets obtained through trade have a dollar value and should be considered as currency. Giving trade tickets to friends and relatives is still theft; they have value just like an admission sold at the front desk. Every admission has an associated expense and impact on your finances. Make sure the trades are good for both parties. Examples of good trades might be prizes for contests, lifeguard retention gifts, and entertainment. The possibilities are only limited by your imagination.

Coupons

Coupons, like season passes, are often misunderstood in this industry. Coupons and online couponing companies like Groupon can work to your advantage if well-timed for your needs, but be careful of overuse. The larger water parks and amusement venues have the marketing dollars and volume to discount with coupons. They have the ability to partner with others such as soft drink companies to subsidize deep discounting.

Here are a few rules when it comes to couponing.

- Never give discounts during your prime season.
- Be sure to number your coupons and record the distribution source so you can evaluate whether you want to use that source again in the future.
- Keep track of the total number of coupons redeemed so you can assess the total value you offered. Use numbers, letters, or codes to track where the coupons were purchased or picked.
- Distribute coupons within your fringe markets—places where you can gain new customers.
- If you want to use coupons, be sure to consider your general admission pricing as you determine the coupon value. If you have a low admission price and then offer a coupon, are you still covering the cost of operation per visitor or even the cost of visitor acquisition?

Smaller facilities have sponsorship, trade, and coupon opportunities, but they are usually local in nature. Partnering, for example, with a local movie theater to honor your aquatic center pass for a discount on a rainy day is brilliant. In turn, the theater may have ads running on your closed-circuit TV or have a display ad on one of your attractions. It's much easier to negotiate with locally owned businesses than with national chains.

The worst public relations issue with couponing is that the visitor never believes your true price or value. There is nothing more irritating than waiting in line and realizing that everyone else has a soda and gets a discount you didn't know about. Constant discounting of your admission price can devalue the actual ticket value. Save your coupons and special promotions for shoulder seasons and times when your facility is empty, but use caution: All that discounting could cost you a new unhappy guest.

Rain Checks and Gift Certificates

Frugal aquatic facilities hate to give rain checks. Public pools almost always have a rule against them, yet rain checks can be one of the best marketing tools at your disposal. Having rain checks available for your management staff's discretion is a great tool for keeping guests. Rain might cancel an outing for guests soon after they arrive. Offering rain checks in this situation can keep the peace, and many times they are redeemed in small percentages so your facility isn't losing out on revenue—and in fact, the goodwill you spread can be a tremendous benefit. Rain checks (sometimes called *splash backs*) can also be a great tool when things haven't gone just right that day at your facility. For example, perhaps it's the day the toilets weren't cleaned properly. An angry mom and a dirty toilet are a dangerous combination, but a splash back or a two-for-one coupon can calm the storm and make a new friend. Apologize, offer another visit, and move on!

Empower your employees to welcome guests back with a splash back pass should their visit not have been stellar.

Gift cards and gift certificates are in the same family as rain checks and coupons. They are a great way to bring in cash during the off-season, and less than 100 percent will usually be redeemed. Consider them as marketing tools for fall and winter press releases and campaigns.

Spectator Fees

You may have guests who want to enter your facility to spend time with a paying patron but don't want to get into the pool themselves. Some facilities may charge a spectator fee in this case, which is priced less than regular admission. Spectator fees are discouraged because guests may try to take advantage of them as a way to pay a reduced fee. Keep in mind that everyone who enters your facility is your responsibility. We protect our guests in and out of the water. While it may be true that Grandma does not swim herself and truly does just want to watch grandson Johnny, she's a liability as much as any other guest.

That being said, there may be times when you need to empower a manager to make an exception for spectators, such as for a religious or cultural issue. Guests with unique needs who come with a caregiver should get a free pass for that caregiver, who will be the one-on-one companion for the guest and reduce your requirement to provide care. For this purpose, offer an unadvertised rate or consider a complimentary admission, but don't publicize it. It can be handled on a case-by-case basis.

Slow but Steady Go the Prices

No one likes to raise fees, but expenses will rise over time. The best practice is to plan on annual increases to gradually and responsibly raise your rates. Be constantly aware of the competition for the leisure dollar, and ensure that your staff members continue to provide good service to every guest. Reasonable guests understand reasonable increases. If guests value your facility, they will equate that value to their admission.

Lessons Learned

- Always work with an experienced financial feasibility firm. If they specialize in a business that isn't related to aquatics, look for someone else.
- Use the cost of a movie as a comparison as you create your fee structure. How do those two hours of entertainment relate to your value?
- Season passes are not money makers, but they can infuse cash during the winter season.
- Sell season passes only prior to your peak season.
- Never sell July for half price. Sell August or your shoulder season.
- Coupons should be treated like cash. Track them to make sure they provide a benefit to your facility.
- Rain checks can be a great marketing tool and a way to create goodwill with your guests.
- Trade admissions for marketing. Don't underestimate your value.
- Continue to enhance your entertainment value, and your perceived value will follow.

PART III

GUEST COMMUNICATIONS

Courtesy of Gretchen Masterfano.

7

GET THE MOST OUT OF MEDIA

In 1964, Marshall McLuhan, author, professor, and marketing expert, introduced a phrase from his widely known book, *Understanding Media: The Extensions of Man* (1994), that has been a point of debate in journalism and broadcasting classrooms around the world: "The media is the message." This phrase has never been more appropriate than today with social media and other advances. McLuhan's famous quote has been interpreted by many. Rob Price (2016) explains the quote to mean that "the form of a medium embeds itself in the message, creating a symbiotic relationship by which the medium influences how the message is perceived." McLuhan said that "a medium affects the society in which it plays a role not only by the content delivered over the medium, but also by the characteristics of the medium itself" (McLuhan [1964] 1994).

I have wondered what McLuhan would have thought about Facebook. Facebook as a media outlet has changed how the world communicates and how news is shared. It has also created an immediate news cycle that often can be incorrect. Fake news not only influences the political front but also has greatly changed how our customers learn about us.

I dreamed of being a journalist as a child; I have always been fascinated by the news and how it is delivered. I did find myself, later in life and purely by accident, in the news business. I had my five minutes of fame in regional television and later in talk radio, causing me to reexamine McLuhan's famous quote. As a college student, I thought that the media consisted of radio, television, print, and Internet. I then surmised that the message was the actual content. I, like others before me, assumed that the medium was more important than the message or content. But only since watching the evolution of social media and seeing my friends and family hopelessly addicted to Facebook, Twitter, and Instagram have I begun to truly understand McLuhan's thinking. Humans are now more interested in recording their experiences and sharing them with others than they are in fully enjoying or participating in an experience. From sharing photos of meals to recording natural disasters while fleeing them, we are now focused on the medium and the message!

We are inundated with content all day long, but it is the experience that ultimately is the message. We have become a world of people who want and need to share everything. It has almost become a cult-like behavior that is the result of looking at content. Sometimes that content causes action, but most often it is the experience that is more meaningful to society. Much like television brought live news into our homes and desensitized us to violence and human suffering while we ate TV dinners, social media has made us a society of voyeurs and created an open and seemingly shameless society. I share this concept to help you understand that regardless of the medium or vehicle you use to share the mission or vision for your aquatic center, keep in mind the power and influence each of these avenues carries. Those with limited budgets and resources need to choose the forms of media that will best relate to their project and the expected outcome of the promotions.

Although much has changed in the delivery of information, there are still some basics that apply to working with today's media. Things are faster than ever! Deadlines come up more quickly, there is more electronic interaction, and there is definitely more competition for the public's attention. But the ease of distribution of information, the chance of going viral, and outlets such as blogs and podcasts have certainly increased our ability to get the word out to the public. Making it effective is another story!

In chapter 8, I will discuss the use of your website and other visual communications through all phases of your proposed project and ultimately the marketing of your facility. In this chapter, we'll explore the basics of working with traditional media outlets as well as electronic news sources.

What's Your Strategy?

Every media campaign should have a well-thought-out list of media outlets that will hit your target markets. Involve your entire team in the plan. Make an official list so others on your team are clear as to whom you will contact and when. Create a fact sheet and a frequently-asked-questions sheet about your aquatic center. Have your video and photo collection ready before the campaign begins, and create your press packet. Be sure that your press packet has links to your website and contact information. You should never have an event without a press packet and a press table. Treat the press nicely and provide food and drink at events; struggling journalists love a good meal, although reporters from some news outlets are not allowed to accept anything. Be aware that some must refuse even a bottle of water or a swag bag. My best advice is to keep a record of all correspondence with the press and track all media about your project. You need to know how your project or program is being reported, just in case you have to go on the offensive.

I'm often asked how far in advance a media plan should be initiated. The answer depends on how many events you expect to produce up to and including the launch of a facility or campaign. For any event such as a groundbreaking or significant construction accomplishment, start assembling the recommended items months in advance. Provide a series of releases and media contacts four weeks out and then weekly in some fashion until the date arrives.

Should You Call a Press Conference?

Unless your project has become a major issue in the community, the chances of having a press conference that any news media would attend are slim. Instead of thinking about a press conference, think in terms of a press event, construction walk-through, or some other activity that

Courtesy of David Guida.

Be ready for the media with a press table, press kit, and facts.

would lend itself to reporting a milestone or newsworthy event for your project.

Communicating in Difficult Times

Even the cleanest, safest, and best-run aquatic centers need to be ready for the moment when things go wrong; it's not if something bad happens, it's when. The first 24 hours following an incident are critical in order to communicate your action steps with the news and social media outlets. Accidents and incidents in the aquatic industry vary in their severity, but because guests can post photos, video, and comments quickly and sometimes without accurate facts, even the simplest incident can erupt into a reputation-busting attack. Today's social media posts that go viral in a matter of minutes can be more dangerous than the actual incident. When faced with a potentially negative incident, reach out to your media contacts head on, with sincerity and honesty, to help minimize potential harm to your facility. Later in this chapter, we'll also review a crisis communications plan to help you manage each interaction. You can never be totally prepared for every circumstance, but you can practice scenarios and train your staff for the best outcome possible.

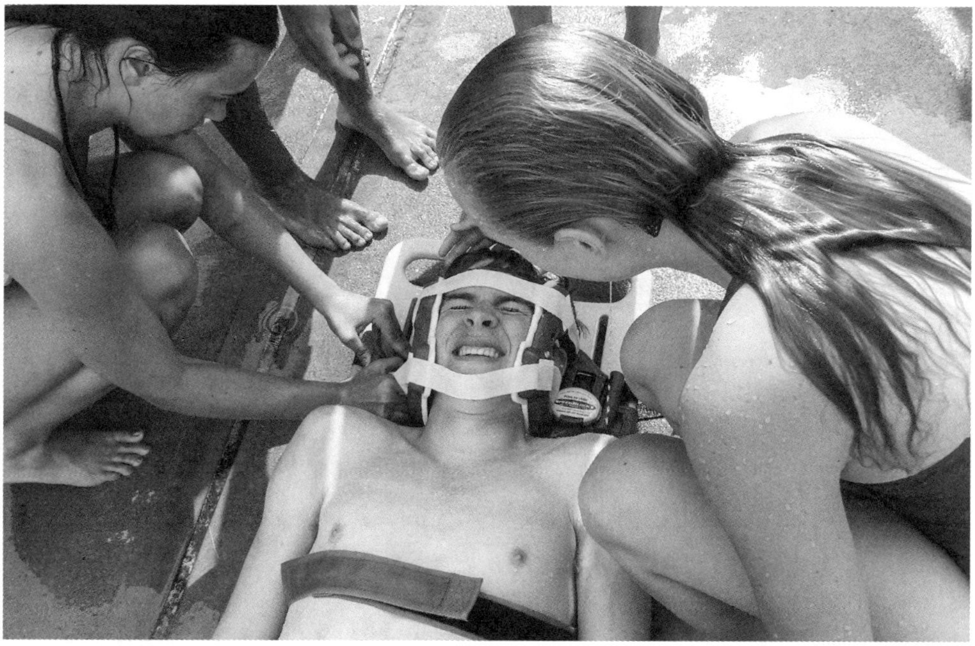

Show your guests your safety team's skills.

Disasters that affect your facility can be caused by employees, members, guests, equipment malfunctions, and natural disasters. Whether intentional or accidental, the scenarios that you practice and prepare for will certainly be resolved more quickly than those that surprise you. Even in unexpected crises, you will certainly perform better if you have practiced similar situations than if you've never even thought through this type of issue before. We entertain thousands of people annually in the aquatic environment, so the possibility of an injury, health crisis, or drowning are obvious things to plan for. But are you ready for a crisis with employees, a food-poisoning incident, or a chemical leak?

Where Do You Start?

Start with identifying areas of weakness and areas where your facility could be vulnerable to criticism. Make a list of possible accidents and incidents from inside as well as outside the organization. Work with the authorities in your community who will be happy to assist with both your emergency management plan and your crisis communication plan. Get them involved especially in those areas that involve public health and safety. Here is a list of things to consider as you develop your crisis communication plan.

- Plan ahead before an incident occurs.
- Make a list of the most probable occurrences.
- Start with simple responses.
- Verify the chain of communication and the proper outlets.
- Be sure to speak with one voice.
- Share information honestly and in a timely manner.

Social media can also play an important role in sharing accurate details, suppressing gossip, and serving as an opportunity for communication between guests and staff. Over the last several years, we've seen how social media has served as a positive outlet for communication through hurricanes, floods, and other natural disasters. When an incident occurs, it is critical that your facility is a vocal participant in the social media conversation. Keep your membership informed of the facts and only the facts. Doing so will also enable you to hear what the public is saying so you can be better prepared for questions and speculation.

A social media interaction following a crisis doesn't end the conversation. Reviewing the information and analyzing the data during the crisis can help your organization be better prepared moving forward.

Share Your Site Plans With Emergency Services

Whether you are designing a new facility or adding a new attraction, your plans should be carefully reviewed by and on file with all the emergency services in your community. Your staff should revisit these site plans annually with first responders. Besides emergency planning, they should know where all entrances and exits are located and the names of the facilities and attractions so they can respond and administer support as quickly as possible.

Develop an Agency Policy

Most aquatic centers have many seasonal employees, many of whom may not understand the severity of an accident and what role they should play in sharing information. Develop a policy that only authorized spokespeople are permitted to speak to the media. Be sure to communicate this policy to all employees, explaining that it is best to speak with one informed voice. Managing and responding to the opinions and gossip of the general public will be monumental in itself; trying to also wrangle dozens of young employees could be almost impossible.

Emergency Management and Media Plan

- Identify the crisis management team (e.g., facility manager, IT services, risk manager, communications manager, human resources manager, maintenance foreperson, security, local police and fire).
- Create the crisis management plan.
- Create a chain of responsibility.
- Identify local emergency services personnel to be activated.
- Create a phone contact list for each scenario.
- Establish a crisis management mission statement.
- Identify possible crisis scenarios and who should be notified.
- Create a list of significant stakeholders who should be notified.
- Create a time diary and call list of those stakeholders for your files.
- Formulate a phone contact list for news and media outlets.
- Assign who will communicate with the media.
- Create a time diary for media communications.
- Create a policy for elected officials, and train them on their response (public facilities).
- Create a contact center with a phone bank for immediate response.
- Include crisis management media policy for staff in the lifeguard and staff manual.
- Have a crisis management consultant and mental health practitioner available for staff affected by emergency.
- Create a template for press releases and social media posts.
- Assign who will communicate with internal stakeholders.
- Detail the follow-up press and public announcements.
- Create a forum for evaluation with a postcrisis evaluation form.

Show Off Staff Skills

The best way to recapture the confidence of your guests with regard to security in the event an incident occurs is to show off your staff members and their abilities. Guests love to see lifeguards practice their drills. Scheduling AED demonstrations and highlighting your staff's qualifications will also create a sense of security. If and when an incident happens on your property, guests will respect your staff's direction and leadership.

Stuff Happens—Then What?

Aside from serious situations, there are those issues that can lead to a disgruntled guest. That guest tells other guests, and before you know it, everyone's talking about a minor problem that just wasn't addressed. For example, even the best-kept facilities may occasionally have a dirty bathroom. When a guest complains about it, what is your staff empowered to do?

The most important skill to develop in our staff is the art of listening. Most complaints can be resolved by listening to the customer, making note of the complaint, and providing a sincere apology to help the guest feel heard and acknowledged. But, there are times when a free return pass or a rain check is needed to fully resolve a customer complaint. Many aquatic managers fear giving a pass or refund, viewing the cost as a problem. Is it worth an eight-dollar day pass to calm what could be a social media mess? I'd say it is!

We are good at documenting first-aid requests and staff behaviors, but are we as good at recording complaints, investigating them, and then responding to our guests? I think not! But we should. Sending a follow-up text, email, phone call, or personal note can earn you a customer forever. We can learn more about our guests' priorities and needs and how we can better serve them. Document the complaint, how it was resolved, and any lessons learned. The time and energy will be well worth it.

Guests spend two thirds of their time out of the water. Teach them, entertain them. It increases your perceived value. Lifeguard demonstrations like this one are just one of many options for guests to get involved.

Dealing With Difficult Conversations

People think that good communicators are born, but that is not true. It takes practice, practice, and more practice. Be sure to dedicate in-service training time with the entire staff to teach how to engage in difficult conversations through role-playing. Training your staff to be some combination of firm and gentle and to find a balance between communicating something difficult and being as sensitive and respectful as possible isn't easy. Here are some tips to help your staff deal with difficult situations.

- Get as much information as possible. Inquire, and don't lose your cool.
- Know what you are going to say and why.
- Remove the person to a quieter place away from the pool deck, such as an office if possible. Crowds help fuel an argumentative guest.
- Be understanding. How would you feel in the guest's shoes?
- Try to problem solve by asking the guest to tell you what she needs.
- Don't back down; don't change your mind unless you are truly convinced you should.
- Remember that you don't have to win every argument.
- Watch your body language. Keep eye contact, and try to sit or stand in a relaxed posture. Listen, listen, and listen more. Stay calm, and tell the person that you hear her.
- Consider asking another manager to join you.
- Negotiate an ending that is mutually respectful and beneficial.

What Media Sources Are Available?

Television and radio offer many opportunities to get your message across. To take advantage of them, you need to plan ahead, have your materials prepared, and become a great source of news and commentary.

Television Airtime

Stick to the regional and local stations, which offer a much better chance of coverage. Save your appeals to the large-market stations for the big stories of regional or national exposure. If you become a great news source or a local expert in all things aquatic, for example, you'll be surprised how often you will be called upon at all levels of television and radio. Even if you can't address a certain subject but can point news directors toward a better source, you'll be shocked at how often they reach out to you. Remember that all press is good press. For example, a drowning incident in your state might become a story on the evening news. Instead of shying away from the topic, embrace it by offering tips for keeping children safe in and around the water. Suggest places to go to learn to swim, and be sure to mention your facility too! Those of us who have grown up in public service tend to shy away from those opportunities, but I say embrace them without embarrassing others. It will take you far.

Become a viewer and listener. Before you spend any time identifying your news and promotion outlets, be sure you want to work with them. This is especially true if you choose to buy airtime. Who watches or listens to the stations? What format do they play? Who is their target market? There have been many incidents of water-park advertising in markets that didn't attract their target market but did bring in folks who did not honor and respect the facility.

- Public service announcements (PSAs) are required for all television stations. They are not typically aired in prime time, but they are exposure. Offer to your local station to tape a PSA at your facility. Better yet, work with organizations like the WWA and buy canned PSAs to which you can then add your tagline or message. It's easier for stations to use your PSAs than to produce their own. Thirty seconds is a standard time to shoot for.
- Community calendars are especially helpful and usually free. You can advertise events that could translate into a story at a later time.
- Viewpoint segments and editorials are few and far between these days with the cost of television time rising. If your aquatic center is a hot topic, you could pitch the station manager or news director to allow a board member or supporter to appear in an editorial segment. Do not do it yourself. The best advice is to never make yourself the face of the project. That's as good as putting a target over your head! Many a parks and recreation director has learned that the hard way.
- Become a panelist or go one on one on a weekly public affairs show. This is achievable in smaller markets if you have something valuable to share. These are usually run on weekends on public television stations and don't have mass appeal, but again, you are on a budget and all exposure is good exposure.
- Have you dreamed of having your aquatic center on the evening news? I can guarantee you that if something goes seriously wrong, you'll get coverage! But, you can get on the local or regional newscast if you have a topic that is timely, controversial, or touching. Weekend news is usually lighter for news assignment editors, so pitch for the weekend.

Television and Video Interview Tips from a Pro

- You can never win an argument against the person who controls the microphone. He has a mute button, and you don't!
- If you need facts and figures during an on-air interview, make a cheat sheet on an index card. Don't depend on memory—it often fades when the on-air light goes on.
- Create a fact sheet or short news release, and send to the host ahead of your visit.
- Prepare a list of sample questions for the interviewer, but don't expect her to use them or ask them in order.
- Never dictate your agenda.
- Never wear white, checks, or busy patterns on television.
- Isolate yourself if you are doing a phone-in interview. Turn off the radio and eliminate any distracting sounds.
- Listen or watch the show before your appearance. You need to know what to expect. Be prepared.
- Talk directly to the host. Don't talk to the audience, and ignore all outside stimuli.
- Check your posture, hair, and teeth before taping.
- Be flexible. Television tapings are stop and go. Live television is not. Be overprepared and hope the pertinent issues are covered. Summarize at the end of the interview, and plug your website, email, or phone number.
- Whenever possible, go into the studio. Talking in person is much more natural.
- Practice your visualization skills. Think it, imagine it, and do it.

- Whom should you know in television? Check out stations' websites for promotion directors, news directors, assignment directors, and sales managers; they'll be listed there.

Radio Airtime

Radio also has responsibility to air PSAs. The same techniques for television PSAs apply to radio. You may be able to get more time on local and regional radio stations. They are more likely to help you produce a PSA, especially for municipal or nonprofit campaigns and projects. Radio also shares community calendars that will provide some exposure.

- Look toward the all-news or talk-formatted radio stations. They have hours to program with shrinking operating budgets. The only problem is that radio listenership is falling. However, local radio still reaches certain segments of the community. Learn their audience and pitch them accordingly.
- Radio talk shows on a local or regional station offer the best chance of free airtime—if you have something valuable to add or can provide entertainment or controversy to the show. Again, listen to the show to understand its slant and get to know the host. Offer up tickets or passes to your aquatic center or invites to a ticketed special event. In radio and television, this is called *trade*. Trade tickets for the station to use for prizes, and you get a mention with every contest. You are also more likely to get an interview if you have provided trade or have purchased some airtime.
- Remote broadcasts will most likely cost money. Although local and regional stations will offer some free remote broadcasts at nonprofit or municipal events, they most often come with an advertising package. Offer them a great remote experience where they broadcast from your property, and perhaps they'll throw you a freebie! Remember that these are business propositions for both you and the radio station. What can you offer them that will increase their listenership or promote their station? Who would be their new audience should they come to your facility for a remote? You have to come prepared with these types of facts and figures to make it work.
- In radio, you need to create a relationship with the promotions manager or, in small markets, the radio show host. At this level, it's all about relationships and opportunity for both you and the station. Be sure your ask comes with benefits for both parties.
- Always assume you're on the air! Say what you have to and stop. Don't feel compelled to fill any quiet seconds.
- Tell a story. Talk radio thrives on it.
- Whom should you know in radio? People include the promotions director, program director, sales manager, news director, weatherperson, and community bulletin-board manager.

Newspapers and Print Media

Throughout the United States, the newspaper business is struggling. Ad sales are down and readership is at an all-time low. With so many other choices, the advertising dollar has diminished, and in turn, the rising costs of labor and production have shifted newspapers to electronic versions. If you want to reach empty-nest readers and older people, traditional print newspapers may still be a successful medium for you.

- News stories are still the backbone of most news publications. Providing news releases that are timely, interesting, or controversial is the key to success in newspapers. In high school you were taught the who, what, and where for news stories, and those principles still apply. Many public agencies think that an announcement about a new class is newsworthy, but the newspaper may not agree. Your small local paper may run that story on a new type of water exercise program, but the real story would be about how it changed someone's life or how it helped an injured veteran. Now that's more newsworthy and could grow into a feature article.
- Features are a real prize in print media, and you will score big if you can make one happen. Again, remember that emotion, relatability, and local impact do make a difference when an editor is searching for the next feature.
- Specialized reports or news series are prime targets for your participation, but you have to know the newspaper, understand its political leanings, and be a good source of information. This relates back to my advice of becoming a local source of information. Offer up not only an idea for a series but also the people or topics as resources. Put together a series about how swimming has changed people's lives. How about a series on the shrinking availability of swimming lessons and rising drowning rates of minority children? Now that's something a newspaper will really get behind.
- Get to know a columnist with your local paper and keep offering stories. You will need to develop a thick skin because you may pitch many ideas but few will make it to print.
- Opinion pages and letters to the editor are best left to your elected officials or board members. Keep your opinions to yourself. It's much safer that way. Don't respond to a fanatical, political letter to the editor. You won't win! Let the process work. You may be surprised at the great response you will get from your supporters. If you do submit an opinion or editorial, keep it short—no more than 1,000 words for sure. Include a cover letter and a short list of the author's credentials. Letters to the editor should be short and to the point. You want people to read them. When possible, meet with the editorial director of the paper. Choose some key stakeholders to bring along, and let them do the work. It's harder for an editor to dismiss you when you meet in person.

- Remember that you are never off the record! Be brief and concise. Give an editor or a reporter something that can be turned into a sound bite.
- Whom should you know in the newspaper business? Important people include the city desk, assignment editor, features editor, sports editor, director of advertising, and electronic media editor.

Online Media

The need for local information will never change, but the way it is produced and presented certainly will. We have seen great movement from printed media to online media, including on cell phones. Online advertising is skyrocketing, local print newspapers are shrinking, and blogs are at risk of containing gossip and unfounded facts. That leaves the responsibility for local news coverage to online sources. Outlets that capture the local market are going to be your best bet in getting media coverage. Online news sites also provide community calendars that can offer free exposure.

Some of the ways for getting coverage by local online press and the recommendations made earlier in this chapter are the same. One change is that things have to be shorter, concise, and visual in order to be effective online. Mike Shapiro of TAPinto.net—one of the fastest growing online local news franchises in New Jersey—offers the following tips for getting online. He's been kind enough to share them with me.

- Make your press releases short, and lead with the story, not your brand.
- Your headlines should be short.
- Lead your story with the *Why*?
- Use subheadings when needed.
- Use videos, photos, and graphics.
- Don't use more than one to three hyperlinks per release.
- Don't create releases that are blocks of paragraphs.
- Have a call to action in the first one to three paragraphs.
- Submit it via email to each reporter or news source.
- Once you submit it online and it's published, push out your link via social media.
- Photo resolution should be at least 100K or higher for online publications, with a minimum of three to five MB.
- Never take photos from other publications. Beware of copyright infringement.

- Provide only the best photos. Don't send them all.
- If children are in the photos and can be tagged, be sure to have their parents' permission. Make sure their names can also be used.
- Video submissions should be meaningful and emotional if applicable.
- Videos should be less than two minutes, ideally 15 to 30 seconds.
- When possible, embed the video links in the content you submit.
- When using online news sites, your ability to link to Facebook and other social media grows your exposure.

Used courtesy of Mike Shapiro, TAPinto, www.tapinto.net.

Lessons Learned

- Practice your responses to a variety of emergencies.
- Be sure to engage social media throughout an issue.
- Drill your staff on your crisis communication plan.
- Show off your staff's abilities to instill confidence and respect.
- Listen, listen, and listen more than you talk.

8

MAXIMIZE ELECTRONIC COMMUNICATION

Some will say it has never been easier, faster, and more effective to reach customers since the creation of the World Wide Web. On the other hand, I feel it has also never been more time consuming, challenging, and cumbersome. This chapter will help you maneuver through this rapidly changing environment and get the most out of your investment of money and time.

Photos and videos have never been more important than in this electronic world in which we now live. When competing for the attention of the public, fast-paced, heartwarming, and exciting photos and videos will grab interest. If you are working with an electronic newsletter, photos are essential to getting the reader's attention. Although posters, signs, and fliers are now considered less effective, photos can still play an important role in paper promotional pieces. Our phones now serve as our computers and our televisions. You can watch a full-length movie on a cell phone while in an airplane flying thousands of feet in the air. With two feet on the ground, your potential customers are looking for entertainment. Photos and videos are the key to getting and keeping that attention.

Whether you believe that the Internet was invented by Al Gore or that it was a conspiracy by the federal government to communicate things without the public knowing, you have to agree that it changes faster than the weather. Each day there is a new app or web format that appears and ultimately disappears again just as fast.

Those of us with limited marketing budgets or no marketing budget at all see the Internet as a solution to our marketing and promotional needs. For some in the parks and recreation world, getting those in leadership positions to understand our website needs, as well as the time and energy involved in establishing a website, is a monumental task. Having crashed a few municipal websites with pictures, videos, and animation, I know a thing or two about what to do and what not to do. I'm happy to share what I've learned to help you to avoid the same pitfalls.

Your Website

If you have to cohabitate within an organizational website, try your best to negotiate your own site that is seamlessly linked to the main site. This will enable you to be more creative; work with photos, videos, and animation; and not be limited to static or outdated sites.

I am not a technology whiz, but I do know what people need and want to get from the Web. For many of us, our first attempt at a website is to tell people everything we know, not just what they need to know. There is nothing more frustrating than going to a website to find something simple like a phone number or a weather alert for a concert cancellation and having to scroll through an electronic version of a brochure or program booklet. Until you ditch that mentality, you will invest hundreds of staff hours on a website that needs constant attention and bores the audience. It also doesn't translate well into mobile applications. Today's busy families don't have lots of time to search the Internet for details such as program cancellations. If they can't find it quickly, they will give up and just not attend.

People go to websites to take away something. That may be information, a call to action, a coupon, or a special offer. Basically, the Internet is a research tool. With the right presentation and approach, the researcher can become your customer. All the rest is window dressing and an attempt to send visitors down the rabbit hole to learn more about your agency and its offerings. Your site needs to be intuitive and fun by incorporating all the work you have done on building your brand.

In the world of parks, recreation, aquatics, and leisure pursuits, the head of the household or key decision maker is usually Mom. Remember that as you design your website. Sure, there are other, smaller target markets for your program offerings, but you can't successfully cater to them all. Quick access to information, photos, and an emotional connection to the brand is what matters most with the mommy market. I dig deeper into what drives that market in chapter 5.

Why Will People Come to Your Website?

It seems like a no-brainer, but asking why people come to your website is a question you must ask yourself. Even if you currently have a website up and running, keep asking yourself, "Why do we have one?"

To Buy

One answer is to convince people to buy from you. For those of us in public life, or operators of small aquatic centers, we want to sell our product, mission, or vision.

The process of selling something is multilayered. You have to have a product. You have to let people know about your product and then persuade them they need it, want it, and should buy it. Once they are ready to purchase your product, you have to close the deal. I can't teach you how to establish an e-commerce site, but you should at least create a simple link from your website to your registration or an e-commerce site for program registration or purchasing tickets. Don't make your customers leave your site to make a purchase. Once they leave, they may not come back.

To Research

Consider this: Someone drives by your beautiful aquatic center and sees a sign. Even though you may have your phone number or address boldly on the outside of the building or on a billboard, the driver will not write down that number. However, he will go online to research your facility. Or, if he overhears a conversation where someone is bragging about your facility or services, rather than ask that person, he will look online to find you. Be ready with the information in an easily digestible format, and he will become a customer.

To Compare

When making a decision about how to spend their leisure budget, people will visit your website to do some comparison shopping. How do you stack up dollar for dollar with schedule, amenities, cleanliness, and more? They will judge your brand and look for a place that earns their trust. First, they will compare your website against those for similar facilities, and then they will head to Facebook, Yelp, and other sources. The content, photos, and design elements are there to seal the deal. Again, it's about research and making an emotional decision.

Understanding what matters to your target market is essential for your success in most areas of operation but particularly on the Web. Safety, cleanliness, and affordability are the top reasons a consumer considers your aquatic facility over others. Does that come across on your website?

To Win or Be Recognized

When developing a marketing strategy for your website, understand that you may have to drive activity to your site. Are visitors in search of a coupon or special offer? Are they entering a contest? Are they looking for the results from an event that can only be retrieved by going to your site? Keep this in mind as you develop your site. Following are a few ideas I have found to be effective.

Beautiful Baby Contests

This has been one of my all-time favorites to drive activity to a website or Facebook page. Get local or corporate sponsors to provide prize packages with babies in mind; this keeps your costs down so your investment is limited to staff time. Ask members and visitors to submit photos of children aged two and under at play at your facility. Award first-, second-, and third-place winners. Be sure to put a disclaimer that any photos submitted for the contest will become the property of the facility and can be used in future promotions. The photos must be identifiable as having

Courtesy of Sophie Mannaerts.

When you come to understand the nuances of each of your target markets, you can create an environment that attracts all.

been taken at your facility. Post the submitted photos and encourage online votes for the cutest baby. If you're doing the content on Facebook, the winners are those with the most likes. Post the winners online and drive the activity back to the website or Facebook page. Everybody loves a beautiful baby. With this kind of contest, you hit a big target market for aquatic facilities and make some friends along the way.

Say Cheese! Cards

If you take photos of guests at your facility, either at a special event or anytime, hand out a cute little card that says, "Say Cheese!" Include your website address on the card, and post the photos in your online photo gallery within 24 hours. Guests will go to the site to see themselves. Just be sure to get permission from people before you photograph them.

Show Us Your Snowman Contests

Much like the beautiful baby contest, this one is a perennial favorite of mine. The marketing of your aquatic center, be it an indoor or outdoor facility, needs to be active all year long. Conduct a Show Us Your Snowman contest, and offer a prize of $100 off a seasonal membership at the aquatic center. The snowman can be built anywhere, but the photo must include members of the participating family. The family that receives the most likes and shares wins the prize, which will drive voters to the Facebook page. Family members and friends from around the world can view and share the family's snowman, driving up the likes and shares. At the same time, it raises awareness of your facility during a season when outdoor swimming is certainly not front of mind. For indoor aquatic facilities that are open all winter, the same contest can be tweaked to include instructions for participants to theme their snowman to reflect current programs. This will drive people to your website or Facebook page and keep you top of mind even in the off-season. You are sure to gain at least a member or two.

Look for Clues

This contest involves giving one clue each week to solve a mystery. The goal is to collect all the clues and win a prize. You can use facts about your aquatic center as the clues. This helps people become more familiar with your facility and creates some buzz during seasonal downtimes.

My Favorite Photos

To build an arsenal of photos from your facility, let members do the work. Ask members and visitors to submit photos, and use your website to show off the best ones. Be sure to include the disclaimer that you have the right to use the submitted photos in your promotions. Everyone who submits a photo gets entered into a drawing for a season pass, guest passes, or some other incentive.

Historical Photos

Everyone loves Throwback Thursdays on social media. Adapt it to your website by asking for historical photos of your facility. Create a page on your website that includes photos taken back in the day. It's a double benefit: You build the historical details on your website, and you drive members and guests to the site.

From the Tower

Instead of just displaying the head shots of your staff, create a column or section on your website about your lifeguards called From the Tower. Everyone has favorite lifeguards, but often they know very little about them. Feature a lifeguard every week, or several per week, with an interview and photos. Young admirers will go to the web page to see their favorite lifeguard.

Website Design

There are some secrets in website design that make total sense once you know them. People who visit amusement parks or water parks may find that the lines on the right are usually the longest, while the lines on the left are shorter because people go to the right first. Some of these types of behaviors apply to website design as well.

- The top left corner gets attention first. Eyes go from left to right, back to left again and right. Visitors typically end their page view in the lower right corner of the site. The lesson is to place key information in the first and last places visitors look in order to maximize the chance they will remember that information.
- Start with larger copy to get visitors' attention, and then you can reduce the size as they scroll through the site.
- Optimize your site to rank well in search engines whenever financially possible. Most people don't look beyond the first search results. Be sure to use the right keywords on your landing page.
- The most important content is above the fold. Make sure the information on top hits the reader with an event, a special price, or a headline.
- Larger images are better than smaller ones. With cell phones performing so well these days, there is no excuse for clip art. Photos gain attention.
- Big headlines get big attention. Save the big headlines for important propositions.
- Just like in dating, first impressions are everything. It takes less than a second for a person to form a first impression of your website. Your logo is a top item to draw attention, followed by the navigation menu. Keep both simple.

Website No-Nos

Think about what you hate about other websites you have visited, and *don't* do it to your visitors. Perhaps you are so overwhelmed by creating a website that you try to use all the tricks in the book. The most important thing is to avoid annoying people. But, some highly paid marketing firms still insist on doing these annoying things. I urge you not to repeat those same mistakes. In some lines of business, perhaps the psychology of an annoying site works. Our target markets want fewer hassles in finding their way to a relaxing experience. Driving them crazy on your site is a real turnoff.

Here are things that drive me crazy, and believe me, it's often a short drive! Avoid these website problems whenever possible.

The landing page is confusing or tedious.

It's all about the landing page. This is where visitors can find out the latest about your aquatic center. If your facility is affected by the weather, having a crawl on top or bottom is important. Weather closings, water temperatures, and operating hours are crucial, and guests need to find that type of information quickly and easily.

It takes too long to load.

I hate that spinning wheel. According to KISSmetrics (Work 2011), 47 percent of consumers expect a web page to load in two seconds or less, and 40 percent abandon a website that takes more than three seconds to load. They will only blame you, not their Internet provider.

It's not readable.

When designing a website in-house, be aware of your font and color choices. Certain colors are tough to read, especially on mobile sites, and people often use their phone in varying levels of light. Just as in signage, certain colors aren't received well by the human eye. Choose carefully.

It's not mobile friendly.

If I can't see it on my phone and get the information I need, the relationship is over. Be sure that any website platform you use is optimized for mobile devices.

Features won't open.

What good is a photo and video gallery that can't be opened by most searches? If people have to download an app to see your gallery, they will quickly leave the site.

Your navigation stinks.

If your navigation is complicated, potential members will check out in seconds. Keep it simple and try to be intuitive. Always design for the new visitor; repeat visitors know about you already.

(continued)

Website No-Nos

(continued)

It uses pop-ups.

It is so annoying to navigate pop-ups when trying to find directions or a phone number. Make your content easy to find and see.

It uses loud musical interruptions.

Don't annoy your website visitors by blasting music when they click on something or reach a certain page. If the noise surprises them, they may leave the site and not come back.

The photos don't match the product.

Those aren't real lifeguards; those are models wearing red swimsuits. Use real photos, and don't try to deceive visitors like a first post on a dating site. If you can't show photos of your facility or employees, at least use good stock photos that are representative of what guests can expect to see at your location.

The Contact Us option only offers email.

Life is full of forms to fill out. Some people want a name and number they can contact to get action now. If a website visitor wants the phone number of the aquatic center to see if it is closed for rain, they will not be happy if they have to fill out a form that gets submitted via email.

Offers are misleading.

Don't hide behind three easy payments or specials that don't exist or that no one wants. You are trying to win people's trust. Don't betray them.

Video Content

Photo and video galleries are vital to your website. It's not about just the photo or video itself but what feeling it evokes. Have you always wanted to swim alone in a beautiful pool? At a public pool, you may never get that chance, but as a sales incentive it works. It plays to your dreams, wishes, and fantasies. Those feelings sell.

Video galleries are important as folks search the web to choose a facility. Videos should always serve you and not just provide information. Do they showcase your vision? Do they represent your brand? Do they

Stay Current

Keep your website and social media pages as evergreen as possible, but understand that they must stay current. Staying evergreen means trying to keep as much consistent information on your page as possible. This requires much less work for you and your staff. Write about your programs, feature photos and videos in generalities, and then have a Register Now button that can take the customer to a registration site with dates, times, and locations. Date changes, price changes, and session dates must be kept accurate. This can be time consuming if you must share every class and program on your website. It's much easier if you keep it evergreen by speaking about your programs offered seasonally and then linking to an e-commerce or registration site that includes important details. Social media can also be used effectively to share up-to-the-minute updates and news.

teach something? Does the viewer finish watching them feeling refreshed, interested, or more knowledgeable? Do they tell a story about your brand?

Using cell phones to film good-quality video and use apps that make editing simple have made it much easier to capture and deliver video content. You can do it! And give thought to how the video is delivered. Rather than using YouTube, I strongly suggest setting up your own version of YouTube. This keeps the content on your site and all about you. If you send members to YouTube to view your video, you are not in control of what video pops up next. In dealing with the family market as we do, this could be dangerous. Keep control of your videos and create your own viewing page.

Get the Analytics

You won't know how effective your online marketing strategy is unless you use one of the analytics apps that are available. Most are free and help show how you are doing. Each year, invite members to come in and help you with a usability test. Give them food and a few prizes, and have them bring their own laptops. Ask them to find certain pieces of information about your facility or department on your website. Watch to see how easily they can maneuver your site or what difficulties they may have. That is your real test by current customers.

Social Media Platforms

Facebook is still widely used, but briefly Periscope was hot, then Twitter exploded, and now Instagram and Snapchat are the choices of millennials. By the time this book is published, the hottest social media platform may have changed. Regardless of the platform, it's important to harness the power of social media for your department or facility. Choose the platforms that best serve your demographic, and do them well. Trying to do them all is too overwhelming. If teens are your market, then Facebook is not your focus; as moms and dads moved into Facebook, the kids moved out. Stay abreast of the latest platforms, and only use those that translate into new or repeated business. If you try to do it all, you will fail. Most of the suggestions for website development and maintenance also apply to social media; just keep it shorter and more photo driven, and don't overwhelm your customers with too many posts.

The best use of social media in our business is for gathering feedback and comments so we know what people are saying about us. Some organizations shy away from Facebook and other platforms because they are afraid of what someone might post about them. That's because those agencies can't handle the truth. I want to know what the buzz is out in the community so I can adjust our operations or work to change negative perceptions. That being said, I caution you to avoid getting into a Facebook war by engaging with someone who has left negative comments on your page. You will not win! Apologize if needed, and offer to speak with the person directly so you can rectify the situation.

Facebook and LinkedIn are two of the most important social networks for marketers today. When asked to choose, most marketers will pick Facebook, especially for the family market. However, many marketing managers are starting to wonder about the effectiveness of Facebook. As it becomes more of a retail marketing site, you may see your numbers drop.

Podcasting is growing in leaps and bounds. It's easier now to produce quality podcasts, and they can be used to cover events, provide interviews with swimmers or officials, and get members to promote your facility by being part of the podcast. Podcasting also allows for immediate feedback. It's all audio. Facebook Live gives both audio and visual contact with potential customers and can also develop a following.

Blogging is a great tool for social marketing, but takes time and energy to keep up. Providing space on your website for a blog will allow you to address topics in more detail, such as safety issues, customer service topics, and just plain entertaining stories of how your facility changes lives.

Using Photos and Videos Effectively

One of my favorite albums of the 1970s was Rod Stewart's *Every Picture Tells a Story*. It comes to mind whenever I talk about the value of photographs in conveying a message to the public. In the same year, I danced to "If," a song that David Gates wrote for his group Bread that rose to the top of the charts. The song starts with a reference to the proverb, "A picture is worth a thousand words." It makes you wonder where the expression comes from and what is behind the meaning. Is it that a picture tells a story as well as, if not better, than hundreds or thousands of words?

No matter the origin of the saying, it remains true more today than ever. As our customers are bombarded with texts, emails, and posts, their attention span diminishes. They need instant connection with your facility. Photos, especially those that evoke emotion, will grab their attention much faster than text. Leisure purchases are made with emotion. We are moved by memories and images of others' experiences, as well as the imagery in our minds of our own search for fun, meaningful experiences.

So Many Photos, So Little Time

At the start of my career, the biggest challenge in using photographs in publications and promotions was the cost of the film development and the printing process. Yes, for those of you who never visited a drive-through Fotomat or rifled through shoeboxes full of prints and negatives in search of just the right photo, you are now spoiled by the immediate and unrestricted creation of photo libraries. With high-quality lenses in most cell phones today and the ability to insert photos into all types of publications, using photos has never been easier.

You have many options for the camera you use to shoot photos to promote your aquatic center. The evolution of camera use for the amateur or hobby photographer has spanned from the DSLR to the point-and-shoot, from the mirrorless to the smartphone. Thanks to the smartphone, we are all much better photographers now, and the photos you use may be yours or those that guests have shared directly or through social media. Everyone is a photographer, which is sometimes a help and other times a nuisance.

A dear friend of mine, Jamie Colucci, a professional photographer and president of Aerial Filming Company, has taught me everything I know about phone photography. In some cases, he feels strongly that the phone lenses are better than most cameras you may be able to afford. Knowing the secrets to taking great phone photos can keep you on budget.

Here are Jamie's tips for great smartphone photos:

- Learn how to crop; don't zoom. Camera phones do not have multiple focal lengths, and zooming will only digitally blow the image up. When in doubt, get closer to the subject instead of zooming in.
- Take a photo at the widest setting, and then crop the photo later for a sharper, undistorted photo.
- Edit your photos; don't use filters. Filters usually make a photo worse.
- Small tweaks to the exposure, contrast, and saturation are OK.

Mother, May I?

In a society of people sharing what they did this weekend, what they ate last night, and who they are dating these days, there are still those who want, need, and embrace their anonymity. For those folks and for the protection of your aquatic center, you must adopt a policy and procedure for photo and video shoots at your events or on your properties.

I have friends in the industry who have learned this lesson the hard way! A young lifeguard's photo appeared on the cover of the agency's annual report. No permission or waiver had been signed by the employee to appear on the cover. Who would have known that he was an aspiring model and had talent representation? The agency knew once the court papers arrived.

Another colleague had taken photos on a busy day at the aquatic facility, and a photo of one gentleman showed up in a local newspaper promotion. It turned out he was on disability leave from work and should not have been riding a major slide. Oops! Who knew his boss would be concerned?

The best approach is to develop a policy to incorporate throughout all facilities and programs. On your registration and membership forms, ask permission to use photos. Post a sign specifying that photos taken on the property will become the property of the agency. I also strongly suggest that before taking a photo or immediately afterward, you get the name of the people who appear in the photo and have them sign a release. If there are children, you will need their parents' permission. Carry a small pad and pencil so you can get their names. Or better yet, have a printed release ready for signature.

Signage and announcements warning folks of photos and videos can certainly help. When possible, take photos of friends, relatives, and staff members who give permission. Take photos of groups, or where it is difficult to identify individuals. Be especially careful of photographing guests and members with special needs. This is often an emotional issue for parents especially. Be sure you know which people from your special needs programs and activities can be photographed.

The Secret Is in the Composition

Choosing how to shoot photos that meet your needs is only half of the equation. Knowing how to best capture the images to tell your story is just as important.

Rule of Thirds

The rule of thirds is used to create the best photos. Imagine you have two horizontal and two vertical lines dividing the frame into nine equal boxes. The rule states that you place your subject at one of the intersections of these lines. Studies have shown that a viewer's eye tends to gravitate toward these intersections rather than the center of the image. Our instinct is to focus on the subject and place it in the center of the photo to highlight its importance, but the rule of thirds makes for a more interesting photo.

Perspective and Angle

Capturing a creative shot also means changing your angle. Consider getting low to the ground or climbing higher than the subject. Take the photo from above or below, or perhaps from behind. A photo of a crowd at a

Courtesy of Sophie Mannaerts.

Create a grid in your mind to get the most out of cell phone shots.

swim meet is far more dramatic if taken from behind the judges' table or at the swimmers' eye level. Change your perspective in your photos, going from wide to close up by changing lenses or your position. Take the same shot in wide, medium, and close-up versions. Be adventurous. If you are shooting digital, there is nothing to lose.

Organize Your Photos

I confess that I am a photo hoarder. I have a problem letting go of any photos. I get emotional and worry that someday I may need that photo. I have been known to keep multiple copies of photos in fear of losing one photo that I could never live without. Some of this mania may have started earlier in my career when photos had to be catalogued in books and slides had to be stored in trays, and there were dozens of boxes of photos under my desk just waiting for that rainy day when I could catch up with a photo diary. Those days are over and I am now reformed—well, almost.

Here's a valuable tip I've learned that I can share with you. Photo folders are limited and will quickly accumulate, making the search for a certain photo on your laptop just as exhausting as rifling through those photo shoeboxes. Use metadata to group images in any number of ways. When paired with catalogue software, you can search for a photographer's name, a location, or a subject to bring together the photos you need. Start with keywords. There's no single right way to keyword a photo, but there is a wrong way. Using the proper keywords depends on who is searching through a collection and what is in that collection. For example, your social media team will search for photos based on who is in the photo, such as Coach Bob. The graphics team will search based on color and lighting, such as pool sunsets or sunny mornings. If you are a team of one, it certainly will be easier, but when working with a team that will need photo access for different purposes, be consistent. Create a list of approved keywords for your team to stay on track.

Storage Is Different Than Organization

You may be familiar with the job of museum curators and their role in maintaining a museum collection. Photo curating is similar but includes capturing, managing, and sharing photos while maintaining the photo record of your agency or programs. Content curation is the process of collecting, organizing, and displaying information relevant to a particular topic or area of interest.

First consider the sources of your photos. You and your staff should top your list. You may have some occasions to hire a professional photographer. You may welcome photos submitted by your guests. The lowest priority should be stock or purchased photos. They may help get you the right photo for a brochure, but using your own photos can be much more relevant. Only use stock photos when you just haven't captured the right shot. If you find it online and use it, so will others. You give away your unique perspective when you use someone else's image to share your vision.

Here are some tips for curating photos that I also learned from Jamie Colucci of Aerial Filming Company.

- Find ways to automate as much as possible, including user uploading, metadata, file conversions, access, and analytics.
- Metadata matters. Structure it wisely. Use analytics to track top search terms, apply keywords and descriptions, and be consistent.
- Use collections for curated groupings.
- Use tags to mark approved or favorite images so they are easier to find and use. Do it right from the start and it won't seem so overwhelming.
- Be deliberate with rights management.
- Document your processes and share with your team.
- Share your curated photos. Include photos in all of your content, social media, blog posts, and so on. Pick the photo that can tell the story with the least amount of accompanying text.

Avoid Losing Images or, Oh, No! My Cell Phone Took a Dive!

While helping a young child get the right fit with a life jacket, I bent over to help adjust the snaps and my phone bounced off the deck and right into the pool. I felt it falling and reached out in what seemed like slow motion to try to save my phone. A Good Samaritan rushed over to assist, but alas, the cell phone shorted out. No amount of drying with a hair dryer, hand dryer, or rice could save my photos. The lesson learned is to always have immediate backup of your phone photos. I had a poorly planned backup strategy and a really good cry! Guess who now has a waterproof phone?

As in sports like football, the best defense is a good offense. Having a solid backup strategy is critical, but the best scenario is to avoid ever needing to use it. There are several steps you can take to avoid losing your data. Real-time backup is the best approach. MacOS users have it made with an automatic backup. Time Machine is practically a dream: You hook up a large, external hard drive and set it to back up all your data. Windows users can consider using Acronis, Mozy, and Backblaze.

Smartphones allow you to adjust the settings so your photos can be automatically saved to a cloud storage platform, such as Google or Dropbox, which are also beneficial because many users can share folders.

A bootable backup gets you back to work right away. Trying to restore two or more terabytes of data can easily take a whole day and is a major inconvenience. Mac users will find Carbon Copy Cloner effective. PC users will find Acronis to be effective.

Offline backup is great when things go only slightly wrong. It gives you a complete cloned copy of all your data. Keep in mind that the data should be easily accessible in case you accidentally overwrite a file or your hard drive fails.

Off-site backup prepares you for the ultimate worst. No matter how many backups you have, you can still lose them all at the same time to fire, hurricane, or theft, so off-site backup is critical. Save a backup in a different location from your working files, such as at city hall or another park location. Clone backup is a decent option and can cover the need for a bootable option.

You've done it all. You have data on your computer (copy 1), you back up at least weekly to an off-line backup (copy 2), you back up biweekly to an off-site backup (copy 3), and you just overwrote the photo you need to send to the newspaper for publication this afternoon. What do you do? Keep redundant copies of data, because all hard drives will ultimately fail. For quick single-file recovery and the ultimate in data backup, you should also have a drive backed up to cloud (online) storage.

Editing and Sharing Tools

Working with photos can be fun when you use tools. Many of them are free and can turn you into a master marketer. Hootsuite is a favorite for managing multiple social media accounts, especially in smaller agencies where one person may be managing all accounts. It helps to correlate all posts. Being consistent across platforms is critical to your success.

Canva is another app that is simple and free. It's a great alternative if you're not trained in or don't have access to Photoshop. Stock photography and graphic design templates are free and readily available. The app fits images to the proper size for Facebook photos, presentations, and more. Canva also provides daily design tips for flier design and layout, email design, design trends, and additional resources. It has tutorials that can turn even the newest photographer into a pro.

Apps like InstaEdit provide different filters and effects. Instagram will help you create collages of up to nine photos at a time instantly or from your photo files.

Video editing apps such as Video Editor can take any video in your photo library and adjust the brightness, contrast, shadows, and more. You can also add music or voice to your videos. Other apps that will turn you into a videographer are Video Editor –Editing Studio and AvFX. Hyperlapse will help you to create time-lapse videos, even while you are in motion, using built-in stabilization technology.

How to Use Your Photos

Now that your photo library is in order, start thinking about the best opportunities to utilize your collection. Keeping in mind that photos will get the most attention in all media formats, plan and schedule your Facebook posts and email notices to correspond with your event and registration timeline. Creating a schedule will keep you focused and can be done during slower times. Knowing what photos are in your file system will keep you prepared when an opportunity arises. Perhaps there is a local news story you can capitalize on with a Facebook post. Remember to get ahead on holidays such as Valentine's Day with just the right photo and story. Some posts should just be for the fun of it! Occasionally use your photos to get an emotional reaction. Photos of the aquatic center taken in the snow or of staff cleaning and preparing the pools for opening day are sure to get attention. Keep stock photos of employees on hand to celebrate milestones or newsworthy stories.

Share Your Photos

Millions of photos and videos are shared in a single day. How will your photo and video shares compete with this deluge of data? How will you stand out? You do not need to be a professional photographer to create a memorable image. It has never been easier to take a great photo. Here are a few tips to make the most of your photographs.

- Use as many social media platforms as you can. Remember that different demographics react to different platforms.
- If you are not using photos or videos to enhance your social media posts or your marketing materials, now is the time to start.
- Always have a purpose to any photo or video that you upload.
- You don't always have to be selling. Upload to inspire and educate customers about your brand or product or vision. Motivate, excite, and post just for fun.

- Powerful images with inspirational messages will appeal to your customers and potential members.
- Double-check for photo bombers, inappropriate backgrounds, or poses that don't represent your products.
- Follow trending hashtags. If you notice a trend, post something relevant within 24 hours or less to keep it relevant. Simple hashtags to follow include #TBT (Throwback Thursday), #Happy, #Summer, and #SharetheFun.
- Facebook and Instagram are only meant to be sneak peaks. Always lead fans to your website to see more.
- Apps make being creative a cinch. There are so many free apps that can enhance your photos with collages, GIFs, slow motion, time lapse, and special effects.
- Encourage fans or guests to create their own videos and post them to your social media pages.
- Get your mascot's point of view by attaching a GoPro video camera to the costume.

Courtesy of Gretchen Masterfano.

Photos of your team will help your guests to identify them when they need them and compliment them as well.

- Tell a story with your images, and make sure they represent your brand. Showcase your employees, recent awards, projects, and accomplishments.
- Be mindful of the message you are sending, and pay attention to composition. It's not always a photo of an event that is effective. How about a child enjoying an activity, with the event as the second layer of the story?

Save Your Energy With a Step and Repeat

Save your energy and bring your subjects to you with the use of my favorite brand tool, the step-and-repeat banner. This is a vinyl banner with your logos, mascots, and sponsor logos as a backdrop for photo ops. Once only used for red-carpet events, this affordable branding tool can be hung at all of your events. The name *step and repeat* comes from the way stars work the red carpet, stepping, smiling, and repeating as paparazzi take their photos. Why not incorporate this great tool at all of your events? It makes for a great background and reinforces your brand. Station your mascot at the step and repeat, and the participants will come.

Thank a Sponsor

One of the best ways to thank corporate sponsors is to provide them with photos and videos of the event they sponsored. Be sure there are photos of the crowd as well as photos of participants interacting with the sponsors themselves. Tag the photos with your sponsors to drive traffic to their Facebook pages. Any video taken that day should also be part of the thank-you video or photomontage. A well-designed video or photo thank-you can later be shown at the sponsors' annual meeting or staff meeting. They will love it!

Bring Your Brand to Life

With the availability of smart TVs and affordable computers today, creating a closed-circuit TV feed is now achievable by even the smallest facilities. Creating videos and bringing your photos to life with online slideshows and in-house commercials can give you a dynamic message to run all day in lobbies, bathhouses, and offices. This is an affordable way to educate the public, promote your activities, and entertain guests while they wait for swim practice or swim lessons to begin. Your message, free PSA safety videos provided by the WWA, and drowning-prevention information can be offered with little technical ability necessary.

Remember, a picture paints a thousand words.

How About Animation?

Things are so very different from when I started in this business. My earlier marketing campaigns used mimeograph machines, a pointed stylus, and stock images that were almost always in black and white or the purple of the mimeograph paper. Fliers and promotional pieces were duplicated on a machine with ink that could make you dizzy. Fliers were run off on a mimeo machine with a huge drum that created a hypnotic sound as it turned. The earlier machines required you to stand by and turn a crank. Now, this was not when dinosaurs ruled the earth; it was only 30 years ago. All the same principles applied, but the choices were limited.

Today, with the use of computers and the great free sites that are available for publishing, when you are developing your logo you must think of animation. Can your logo or mascot be animated in some way to attract attention of the public? Does it call for sound with animation? Perhaps the sound of the waves crashing, kids laughing, or birds chirping can enhance the logo.

At the start of this chapter, I mentioned that marketing has never been easier thanks to the Internet and social networking. I also shared that it has never been harder. I hope I have enticed you to move forward with these two important marketing vehicles. I, however, am tired from even writing the chapter. I think I'll go watch water-park videos online to relax!

Lessons Learned

- The female head of the household makes the majority of the leisure decisions for the family. Understanding the female consumer will result in a healthy bottom line.
- Your website is not an electronic version of your former paper brochure. It has to remain viable and accurate.
- Be sure your media are smartphone friendly. That goes for your registration programs as well. Soon, we will all use our phones more than our computers.
- People like recognition on sites such as Facebook. Contests on Facebook that require likes and shares are effective in building new audiences.

- Be sure your fonts and colors are readable. Frustrating potential customers is not a good way to start a relationship.
- Start your own version of YouTube to control the content you create. It's more family friendly.
- It's not about the photos and videos; it is about the emotions attached to them.
- Don't put your subjects in the center of your photos. Use the rule of threes.
- Save only the best photos, not every one. Digital photography makes this much easier than back in the days of film.
- Catalogue your photos right after an event. This task becomes too large when you wait until you have thousands to file.

9

TURN LIFEGUARDS AND STAFF INTO AMBASSADORS

Courtesy of Gretchen Masterfano.

The most effective marketing and promotions plan can be quickly undone by one bad customer experience at your aquatic center. Marketing experts used to say that one bad experience would be shared with nine others, and in turn those nine would tell another nine, and so on. Those kinds of statistics instilled fear in aquatic operators. Today, that fear is magnified: With the popularity of social media and travel-rating websites and apps, one bad experience can quickly turn into hundreds or even thousands of shares. Before you've had your morning coffee and received your manager's report from the preceding evening, hundreds of potential customers could be lost.

Whether your facility is seasonal or open year-round, you most likely depend on part-time, hourly, and seasonal staff. Your biggest challenge is creating a sense of ownership and loyalty in these employees, with whom you may not have daily or even weekly personal contact. Your facility management, safety team, and maintenance personnel represent your aquatic center to your guests. Turning them into ambassadors who reflect your vision, mission, and philosophy is a real challenge. I've been able to accomplish this with many facilities I've managed, and I'm happy to share some of my hits and misses.

Your front desk and management team understand their role in customer service, but for the most part, the employees who safeguard the guests at your aquatic facility are of an age group that believes it is a generation of master communicators. In fact, nothing could be further from the truth, so it's your job to train them to communicate well with your guests. These days, customer service skills are almost as important as the ability to scan the water and perform rescues. As people determine where to spend their leisure dollars, they are more selective with their purchases. The competition for a family's discretionary funds is fierce. Everyone and everything now matters more than ever. A simple incident shared on Facebook can ruin your facility's reputation.

Turn Your Vision Into Theirs

Many agencies that I have coached or staffed over the years spend an inordinate amount of time developing their mission and vision statements. They hold focus groups on their marketing concepts, website usability sessions, and poolside chats with their user groups, but they often overlook sharing all of this information with their part-time, seasonal, and line staff. If you ask staff members if they know the mission statement, goals, or even the names of people who appear in the organizational chart of the aquatic facility, you are certain to get a cold stare. This is totally understandable. With all of the training requirements, personnel and payroll obligations, and reporting requirements, your quality time with these important employees is rather limited. Successful agencies understand the need to include their seasonal staff members in their vision and mission. Making these employees feel respected and honored is a good start to making them feel like part of the whole organization.

Start with sharing your mission and vision. It may have to be simplified and abbreviated, but at least it is shared. Creating a mantra such as "Safe, clean, happy" for your aquatic center is quick, simple, and easy to understand. Post your mantra, use it in trainings and workshops, and repeat it on signage in all employee areas as a way to make it part of the conversation.

Finding a mantra that best fits your mission starts to tie together the whys of what you do. Many of us working with millennials and younger people may be asked, "Why do we have this rule or that policy?" Using a mantra can help you answer the whys that reinforce your agency's vision. If lifeguards and other members of your team are expected to enforce rules, they need to know and understand why. If they are going to explain a rule to your guests, they need to understand it themselves so they can act as a knowledgeable ambassador.

For example, perhaps your facility doesn't allow food on the deck close to the pools. This may be a requirement of the state bathing code, and lifeguards should know and understand that. Perhaps your state requires reusable swim diapers and does not allow the store-bought disposable diapers. Should lifeguards need to enforce that rule, they need to be able to explain that diapers with elastic legs or training pants will better entrap feces so we can all avoid a code brown or a pool closure. When guests and staff understand the rules, they can better enforce and live by them.

We all understand the importance of in-service trainings to develop lifeguard and staff skills when it comes to rescues, scanning, and crowd control. But, how do we develop well-rounded lifeguards who can also be goodwill ambassadors at our facilities? Gossip, bad information, and teenage speculation can set back your customer service efforts, marketing, and bottom line. In-service training of lifeguards and staff in all areas of customer service should be a vital part of your training plans.

Wear Your Vision on Their Sleeves

If safety is the number one priority at your aquatic center and it is part of your goals, why not literally wear your mission on your sleeve? You can use your own phrase or adopt one from another agency, such as the WWA's "Be Water Aware" or "If Your Child Is in the Water, You Should Be Too" campaigns. You have dozens of walking billboards at your aquatic facility—use the opportunity to share your vision on the sleeves or backs of your staff shirts.

Being a loyal member of the WWA, I wanted to adopt their "If Your Child Is in the Water, You Should Be Too" campaign, but it just didn't fit the community facility I was operating at the time. I scaled the campaign to fit smaller facilities and the community pool environment. With the WWA's blessing, I instituted the "I'm Watching Your Child. You Should Be Too!" campaign on signage throughout the facility and the backs of all our staff. At first, this in-your-face campaign felt gutsy; some staff felt that it could be insulting because guests might feel we were insinuating that they didn't watch their children. However, on opening day the signage and T-shirts met with great approval from our guests. In fact, many remarked that the only people who would be insulted by the campaign were those who didn't watch their children. This safety campaign has now been adopted in other communities, and the T-shirts and logo are available through Water Safety Products at www.watersafety.com.

What better way to exhibit your vision, but on walking billboards?

The campaign continues with the phrase, "We Are the Lifeguards, You Are the Lifesavers." Lifeguards have the ultimate support of the organization and its membership, and they carry this message proudly on their shirts. It gives them a sense of empowerment when it comes to disciplining members and giving direction.

How Do You Instill Compassion?

Provide training for your aquatic staff in meeting the special needs of your guests. Sensitivity training will not only result in the development of compassion for others in the workplace but will also create better world citizens. Don't stop at teaching the staff how to use the ADA lift. Educate about the needs of people of all ages who may need additional assistance in some way. Encourage service that goes beyond the standard. Teach staff how to identify mobility issues on the deck and in the water. Allow for accommodations such as noodles, submergible wheelchairs, and other equipment, and explain why to the staff. Recognize those who go out of their way to make all guests feel welcome. Teach them how to discreetly get assistance or guidance on deck when they are not sure of a member's condition or ability. It's best to be open, honest, and communicative to help a staff member understand how to best serve guests who need special accommodations.

Who Works for Whom?

Many lifeguards and aquatic teams may feel they are out there on an island all alone if they don't feel connected to your agency, city, or ownership. Helping them to understand they are part of a whole organization that provides service will foster an attachment to their facility. Sharing the organizational chart, providing tours and experiences within their own city's facilities, introducing them to city officials, and including them in the agency's services will help to foster this sense of ownership. They can then be better informed when asked questions about your programs and services. Knowing the roles and responsibilities of those above them will help your employees to better understand their role in the agency. This seems simple, but the message often gets lost in the hectic nature of our busy seasons and the quiet of our slower times.

I remember an occasion early in my career when I was the director of a major recreation department in New Jersey. While hosting a VIP reception at a Fourth of July celebration, a young man came to the entrance and asked for admission even though he did not have a ticket. I recognized him as a lifeguard, and I told him that if he could tell me the name of the director, he would get admission. I was standing right in front of him and he could not even guess at my name. I explained who I was and granted him admission. That was an aha moment for me. My agency and I had failed this young man. Granted, this was a large agency with lots of full-time and seasonal employees, but obviously we didn't translate our mission and vision down to the staff. I committed myself to including all employees in any way reasonable and affordable.

Throughout Europe, many aquatic centers cross-train employees so they can work all areas of the facility (e.g., lifeguard, maintenance, front desk, restaurant). This gives the employee an understanding of what it takes to make a facility successful. Now, I am not suggesting we follow that model in the United States, but it does support the concept that everything and everyone matters. Our job as supervisors is to constantly prepare our employees for advancement. Understanding how a facility operates is essential to the development of our future industry leaders.

Employee Empowerment Is No Easy Task

Many of our policies are customer driven, which is important for any operation, but are those policies setting up your management and lifeguard team for success? Is there room to empower your employees to make decisions in the field that can defuse an uncomfortable situation? This can be difficult for those who work for government agencies, where rules and regulations leave little room for flexibility and empowerment. One suggestion is to have representatives of the entire aquatic management team participate in a review of your policies and procedures. Get their input and support. Listen to their issues, especially those related to customer service. For example, there will be times when your rainout policy doesn't fit the occasion. Are staff members authorized to issue a rain check or splash-back credit? Statistically, a high percentage of these credits never get returned, but they foster goodwill with customers. Consider allowing these to be issued with the manager's discretion. Give your staff the opportunity to diffuse complaints and offer a return visit. That small sense of empowerment will not only enhance the customer experience but also make the manager more confident and compliant rather than defensive.

Have you instilled in your lifeguards the confidence that you will support them in their actions when life and safety issues are at risk? Young, inexperienced lifeguards need to know that you will support them when responding to an aquatic emergency, even if it is a false alarm. Young employees may be inhibited by what others will think. Create an environment where safety is paramount and you applaud them for responding, even if their response may have been unnecessary.

Parents can be trying when lifeguards correct their children. Constantly reinforcing that safety is the main priority will give lifeguards the confidence they need to enforce safety rules. Provide lifeguards and aquatic staff with suggested responses, and regularly practice drills related to these customer interactions. Why can't someone run and jump over other kids? There's a good reason for it. Do your staff members know why?

Swim lessons and life jackets save lives. Use your safety partners to help you to deliver the message.

If you provide free life vests and limit life vests to devices approved by the Coast Guard, your aquatic staff needs to understand what those devices look like, how they should fit, and why you provide them. If you have restrictions on hard plastic toys in your family leisure pool, do the lifeguards understand the rule and what types of toys are allowed? These rules are necessary, and staff must understand the reasons behind them in order to be responsive to your guests. This will build confidence and ultimately help your lifeguards earn the respect of guests for ensuring a safe environment.

I'm always shocked at the interpretation of rules and regulations by those who do not write them. Always keep that in mind as you hold in-service training sessions. I once had a lifeguard tell a customer with a child with a skinned knee that we had no first-aid supplies. How could he think that? I brought the lifeguard into the first-aid room and showed him the cabinet filled with supplies. He was shocked and obviously confused. Our standard operating procedure (SOP) for first-aid ointments, creams, and sprays was that our staff did not administer these items, but a parent could. His interpretation was that there were no supplies available. So be aware of the clarity of your language and instructions when training and instructing staff. Sometimes our instructions are heard differently based on the employee's age or experiences, as the following example illustrates. While on the property, a child scraped her toe, and her parent requested a Band-Aid. So I sent a young, eager lifeguard to the first-aid room for a Band-Aid. He returned to me twice and said, "We have no Band-Aids." I told him that couldn't be true, and I went into the first-aid room myself. I returned with a large box of adhesive bandages—a generic version of Band-Aids. This lifeguard didn't see a

I'll Keep an Eye Out for You

Quick-thinking managers can turn any potential problem into an opportunity. Aquatic operators have always marveled at what clothing and personal items their guests leave behind. On a bright and sunny day, a young girl ran into the manager's office with her hand clenched. She was excited by what she had found floating in the water. She told the manager that she had found a marble in the pool. The quick-thinking manager asked her to open her hand. He took the object and told her, "Congratulations! You have won a prize!" He reached into our supply cabinet and gave her a set of goggles. She skipped off feeling happy and excited. Immediately after she left the office, a gentleman with one eye closed approached the manager looking for his glass eye. The marble was something much more valuable. The quick-thinking manager saved the day, preventing what could have been an ordeal for the little girl and the gentleman. Following the event, the expression "I'll keep an eye out for you" became a catchphrase at private staff meetings. All employees need to feel empowered to do what they need to do to get out of a tough situation.

box of Band-Aids, so he was right about that, but he didn't realize that adhesive bandages were the same thing.

Continuous Improvement Through In-Service Drills

Drills to help staff practice how to manage on-deck issues such as bullying, arguments, rubbernecks, code browns, and angry guests are imperative in today's high-stress climate. Tests, drills, and flash-card sessions that cover the rules, regulations, and policies of your facility can be important training tools. In this age of litigation, many of us hand out staff manuals and expectation agreements, but how many of them are actually read? Especially in short seasonal environments, by the time you recruit, train, and uniform these employees, they work for a few months and then go off to sports or back to school. Keep in mind that attention spans today are short. That, combined with memory overload and sleep deprivation, drives the need for in-service trainings that are fun, challenging, and memorable. Hold trivia contests to test knowledge and application of your policies, and award prizes. Offer incentives for those who consistently provide good customer service. Use the salami effect when teaching rules and regulations: Serve it up one slice at a time. Take advantage of overcast and rainy days when few or no guests are present to have discussions about your policies and the reasons behind them.

Remember to give attention to teaching interpersonal communication skills. In some families, the simplest of social skills have not been taught at home. You may have to teach your staff the value of eye contact, the art of the handshake, and other simple social graces. These skills can be taught by you and your leadership staff by example; use every opportunity as a teachable moment. If you believe that everyone and everything matters, your staff and your guests will too.

Uniforms and Rituals: Tools to Develop Respect

The water-park community has come to understand the importance of the appearance of lifeguard staff in gaining the respect of customers and pride among employees. This same commitment to a professionally outfitted lifeguard staff has continued to elude some aquatic centers, in part due to ignorance and financial concerns. In addition to skills training, the professional appearance of a lifeguard should be a priority. Professional uniforms that enhance self-esteem in your employees can

When Funny Is Okay

There are times when humor can be an appropriate response when something goes wrong. My favorite story of using humor to resolve an issue happened to me early in my career. One of my favorite corporate sponsors was inadvertently left off a sponsor list in our weekly newsletter to our members. The sponsor was a dental practice that had been a longtime supporter of our facility. I immediately called the practice and apologized for my omission. They were extremely understanding, but I used humor to turn the situation around. In the next newsletter, I offered a full paragraph of an apology that started out as, "Would you like to find a dentist who is kind, understanding, and patient?" I then went on to explain our omission in the previous month's newsletter and raved about how understanding and patient they were with me. Who wouldn't want a dentist like that? They loved the extra coverage and the humor in the apology. It resulted in a long-term relationship with a great corporate sponsor.

Sometimes there is nothing else to do but resort to humor. Years ago, the state of New Jersey opened the Camden aquarium. The city needed an attraction to help bring tourism dollars into the area. Well-meaning political types felt that a New Jersey aquarium should only feature New Jersey fish species, even though native fish are not very interesting or colorful. After one visit, most guests were underwhelmed and did not return.

This required some new approaches and, of course, more colorful fish. Several people lost their positions, and a new public relations campaign was introduced. It used humor in one of the most hysterical comeback marketing campaigns I've ever seen. Billboards and full-page ads stated, "Fish heads roll at the aquarium. (Remember those dull grey fish? We threw 'em back.)" Another billboard stated, "So, our curator was colorblind. (The new guy threw back those boring grey fish)." And my personal favorites were, "Our gray fish got the pink slip" and "Our fish don't stink anymore." Self-effacing and appropriate humor is a great way to turn around a disappointing campaign or program. People appreciate the humor and humility. The aquarium survived and is a big success today.

make a big difference in their daily demeanor. Are the suits comfortable? Do lifeguards have hats, visors, and sunglasses to help them be better recognized by guests and protect them from the sun? Do you provide whistles, lanyards, water bottles, and other tools to make their appearance worthy of respect? Name tags are especially important in providing good customer service and establishing a personal relationship between your members and staff. Adding information to the name tag such as the school they go to, the sport they play, or a special talent will also instill a sense of pride.

If your guests have respect for your lifeguards, your safety record and staff retention will soar. I'm a big advocate of ritual, especially with young employees. I've been a tireless advocate of the walk-around. When lifeguards are returning to their break area or headquarters, I require them to walk around the main pool of the facility. This little staff parade on the half-hour instills some pride in the staff, helps guests recognize the lifeguards, and inspires respect. Give it a try. At first, the staff may balk at it, but it also gives them the opportunity to interact with the guests, show teamwork, and identify any deck issues.

Whether you have a break room or only a shaded break area, refer to it as the headquarters. If possible, post a sign explaining that this is the lifeguard gathering area. Although on break, they are still on duty to respond to an emergency, swim test, or need for first aid. Giving them a respectable break area and honoring them by calling it their space gives them a sense of ownership that will come out in many positive ways.

One of my favorite rituals of all time is performed by a maintenance staff member. He is a proud Navy veteran, and affectionately called *the Captain*. This senior adult is a hardworking man with a giant heart to match his stature. Each evening at closing, he takes down the American flag outside my facility. He chooses a child who is exiting the park at

Rituals make lasting impressions on guests, especially those that tug at their emotions.

that time to assist him in retiring the flag. He teaches them how to fold the flag and how to raise and lower it, and he gives a quick lesson on flag etiquette. This has been one of the most touching applications of our mantra and vision that I've seen in my career. The Captain obviously understands that any simple act can be an experience that demonstrates our mantra of "Safe, clean, happy."

It Costs How Much?

In addition to taking good care of guests, you want your staff to care for your equipment and facility—and encourage the same from guests. Staff may not realize the cost of the equipment you need to maintain. Here's a personal example that highlighted for me the importance of clueing in my staff about these expenses. I once had a lifeguard who was a bit of a comic. He saw an opportunity to make the staff laugh by drawing a mustache on a Shark Diddy mascot sign at our aquatic center. Because he used a whiteboard erasable marker, he thought his artwork could be easily removed. However, the marker wouldn't come off, damaging a $500 sign. When I expressed my disappointment in his gag and shared with the lifeguard the cost incurred, he was shocked! I learned two valuable lessons from that experience: One is that you can't withhold pay from employees even when they have willfully damaged your property. The second is that employees likely don't understand the cost of the equipment, signage, furnishings, and equipment used in our industry.

Because of that experience, I now play a game with staff called, It's How Much? The right answer gets a prize, but prizes are seldom needed because usually no one guesses correctly! I enjoy their amazement when they learn that a commercial trash receptacle could cost $500, an ADA lift could cost $4,000, a pool vacuum is $2,500, and so on. The game helps staff to realize the expense of running an aquatic facility, and the next time they are responsible for that equipment, they know its value to the agency.

Give Credit Where Credit Is Due

At the entrance to your facility, are there photos of your staff with their titles? Do you post articles about their accomplishments? Recognition goes a long way, no matter what the age or status of an employee. We all understand that, but we often lose sight of it because of hectic schedules and long days. I've seen many successful employee-recognition programs. In one facility, a manager walked around with a bag filled with Life Savers candy. Whenever she saw employees perform above and beyond expectations, she tossed them a lifesaver—tiny gesture, big effect.

Other managers give out beads to wear on lanyards, coins for making purchases in the staff store, bus passes, movie passes, gas cards, and other small rewards. These can be great ways to improve the recruitment and retention of staff. Developing an environment that recognizes accomplishments will increase your bottom line because you don't have to spend as much time and expense in training new staff, and it will improve membership retention because you have happy employees who feel valued. Still doubt how a few wooden beads could be significant to a college kid who drives a better car than you? Try it and report back to me. It's amazing.

Electronic and social media can make recognizing your staff easier, too. You could feature lifeguards in a weekly article called "From the Lifeguard Chair," where you list their school, college major (if applicable), sports they play, accomplishments, and more. These types of recognition go a long way with your team members, especially when they can share them online.

For so many of our young employees, this is their first job experience. Getting that first paycheck is a monumental occasion in a teen's life. Why not celebrate it with a photo of them getting their first check? It will make them feel valued, and the guests will get a big kick out of it. For other staff, it's a manageable summer job in a cool environment. With competition for summer jobs that pay more than you do, how do you keep them coming back? The work experience has to be just that: an experience. Yes, it is an important position with a lot of responsibility, but it also needs to be fun. Involve your staff in planning their own celebrations and social activities. Encourage them to create videos and promotions that they can star in. Host special events just for staff that will remain with them over the winter, bringing them back another season.

Lead By Example

If you believe the core principle behind aquatics is service, you must show it in all you do. Your management staff will set the tone for this at your aquatic center. Managers need constant communication with you to ensure the delivery of your message. If you and your management team understand that everyone picks up papers, everyone pulls weeds, and everyone can fit a guest with a life vest, you are on your way to many successful seasons.

Lessons Learned

- Empower your personnel to handle customer service complaints, and support them.
- Be sure all staff members understand the vision and mission of the agency. They are your ambassadors.
- In-service trainings are as vital for your front desk as for your lifeguards.
- Be sure to explain the whys of your rules, so staff can adequately defend them.
- When you make a mistake with a promotional campaign or corporate sponsor, try to have a sense of humor about it. Make up for the omission and move on.
- From uniforms to daily rituals, all things contribute to your staff's sense of ownership and pride.
- Employee-recognition campaigns work. Be creative and trade with movie theaters, bowling alleys, and area restaurants for gifts and prizes.
- You must lead by example, because your employees are watching you and your managers. Everyone picks up papers, understands the rules, and acts as customer service representatives.
- Cleanliness and safety are still the paramount drivers when people consider joining an aquatic center.

PART IV

MARKETING WITHOUT MILLIONS

Courtesy of Sophie Mannaerts.

10

USE SPECIAL EVENTS AS PROMOTIONS

Courtesy of Sophie Mannaerts.

Programs and special events can increase attendance when planned and executed well. Although most managers see special events and programs as a service to current members and their guests, I've always viewed them as marketing opportunities. The way to get the most value from your hard work is to see these programs and events not only as an obligation to your current membership but as a way to attract new members as well. Sure, they increase the perceived value of your facility, but they are also excellent promotions. Your aquatic center is the meeting place for families in the summer. Why not capitalize on such a great environment?

One mistake many managers make is holding special events on the days when their facility has the highest attendance. This is backward thinking, but I understand it. Parks and recreation professionals are all about numbers. Attendance at events is often the measurement of success. But in aquatic centers, it should be about entertaining current members *and* attracting new members. Special events should be used as a way to fill your facility and to maximize the attraction for your members to bring paid guests. This will help increase your daily revenue and allow the daily guests of your members to try out the facility under the best of circumstances.

Most aquatic centers are filled on the weekends with members and their guests, but how about Thursday after six p.m.? I would guess that numbers through the gate are typically lower during that time. Why not offer a special event or program then? For example, advertise free admission in the evenings, and entice attendees with a special program or event. This will bring people into your facility who might not otherwise come. Perhaps a movie, magic show, or musical act is the attraction, but now someone who hasn't visited your facility in years gets to enjoy it and may be tempted to join. The other benefit of the open-gate concept is that it can give kids and families who might not be able to pay the opportunity to visit your site, especially for those facilities that are not able to offer a scholarship plan. You have fulfilled a moral obligation and provided a service that proves you are a good neighbor and a charitable agency. You will see your attendance and revenue numbers rise not only on the night of the special event but perhaps long-term as well.

Entertaining Events That Promote Your Facility

Municipal facilities and small corporate facilities that have tight budgets may not be able to hire quality musical entertainment or performers. That's OK, because I propose that there's a fail-safe way to entertain your guests without the expense of professional entertainers. Our communities are filled with dance studios, martial arts studios, fitness centers, regional theater groups, amateur musicians, artists, step teams, cheer squads, poets, and more. If you are lucky enough to have a stage or an entertainment area such as a shade structure, patio, or even an entry pavilion, you are on your way to offering community talent showcases. All you need is a flat surface and a portable sound system. The performers get free admission; their friends, relatives, and fans have to pay the entry fee. If you are feeling especially philanthropic, you can offer a buy-one-get-one admission. These types of events will expose people such as grandmothers to a facility that they might never see under normal circumstances. Chances are, they will return and purchase a ticket. Even if they don't, they will talk about your facility among friends and post photos or videos to social media sites; in essence, they do the marketing for you. Allow performers to have an information table or accept donations if your agency allows fund-raising on your property.

It doesn't have to only be about performances. There are many organizations in your community who would love the opportunity to have an information table that's educational and entertaining. For example, the local arboretum could give a class on plants, insects, and the environment. Consider hosting a health fair with your local hospital and EMS. Chiropractors love giving lectures and demonstrations. How about a fashion show from a school or local fabric store? Ladies' nights with massage chairs, hair braiding, and yoga sessions all provided by local commercial and nonprofit providers have all been successful using this model. Provide chairs and a tent, and you have an event.

So why aren't more aquatic centers holding special events like these? I understand that it is difficult enough to operate your facility, but summer interns, volunteers, and seasonal workers are perfectly capable of scheduling these activities and working the performances. For facilities that take this challenge on, the possibilities are endless.

How do these relationships pay off in addition to exposing new potential members to your facility? With Facebook, Instagram, and other social media, it's all about the likes. Partnering with local organizations, businesses, and nonprofits in promoting their presentations and performances will result in exposure, new follows, and likes. These numbers will reproduce daily and provide you with free exposure that is far more influential than a simple display ad or press release. Community-based events often get local or regional news coverage. During slow news seasons such as the summer months, interesting entertainment at your facility will attract attention. Getting local news outlets involved makes for great background video for weather reports on their station. The more unusual the event, the greater the chance is for TV coverage. If you can't

Courtesy of David Guida.

Swim Lessons Save Lives. It's an international effort, one facility at a time.

attract local television, take video of the event yourself and post it to your social media accounts. Who knows; it might go viral!

Show Your Style

Special events are great promotional tools when they show your passion and imagination. If you pump up the volume on your special events with theming and unique partnerships, you have a much better chance of making a lasting impression on participants. The more creative and special your events are, the more buzz you will get on social media and the more likely you will be to get TV coverage.

Presenting themed special events does not necessarily mean they have to cost more. With some creativity, you can theme your special events for the entire season with simple props, costumes, and gimmicks. Under the Sea, Happy Birthday Mascot Party, Swashbuckling Summer, Knights to Remember, Country-Western Fun, and Superhero Summer are just a few ideas that have left my customers wanting more. The value in setting a summer-long theme is the reuse of props, costumes, and promotional items. With themes, you also have the opportunity to work with others who value your imagination. The Knights to Remember appealed to Medieval Times, a themed restaurant chain. They jumped at the chance to be part of the action and sent costumed knights, princes, and princesses to the event, offering coupons and photo ops with the kids. The mascot at the Summit Family Aquatic Center dressed in a king costume and rode in on his trusty steed. The nearby Union County stables heard about the event and welcomed the chance to bring Brutus the quarter horse to the event. He wore a crown as well, and rode in with Shark Diddy (King Diddy that night), to the amazement of our guests. The Union County stables were happy to offer photo ops with Brutus and distribute information about their riding lessons.

Everybody wins when you theme your events. Sometimes, the theme comes to mind first and then the partnerships fall into place, while on other occasions the partnership comes first and then the theme materializes. Watch for trends and world events to help to visualize your themes. The anniversary of a film such as *The Wizard of Oz* can kick off a summer of themed special events that are sure to please. Instagram, Facebook, and other social media platforms explode with photos and comments on the events, especially when photo ops are provided. When your mascot rides into your aquatic center on a horse or poses as a pirate in front of a ship, you are going to get likes on your social media.

Keep up the theme on dry land and in the water. Cannon-ball contests during your Swashbuckling Adventure, with your mascot as the judge, are sure to impress. Take photos with your underwater GoPro, and you

Courtesy of David Guida.

Fantasy becomes reality. Out-of-the-box programming increases your facility's entertainment value.

have a YouTube sensation. Pirate-themed party games, a pirate magician, and a DJ in costume make an event even more memorable. Members and guests see that you care, and they are sure to come back for more. The greatest promotional value gained from this type of creativity is that everyone is talking about your aquatic center. Kids will rave to their friends about how much fun they had. This type of experience is found at private swim clubs and other commercial aquatic centers. Kids are key influencers that marketing firms respect, and the kids in your community are going to insist that their parents buy a membership or visit frequently to be part of these types of events. The condo pool, swim and tennis club, and fitness pools will pale in comparison. Even the large, high-energy parks cannot offer the same level of participation in events like this. Make everything you do memorable, and you will have them clamoring for more.

Always be sure to have a step-and-repeat banner as part of your event plan, as detailed in chapter 8. Every aquatic center or water park should have one. Each photo becomes an instant advertisement. With the ease of sharing photos through Facebook and the web, photos of the event with your logo boldly in the background gives your aquatic center exposure that you could never afford to buy. Give your guests at special events lots of photo opportunities to post on Facebook. They are the best form of free advertising, and something really cute could go viral!

That's Aqua-Tainment!

Now, wait a minute. You are running an aquatic center and you barely have time to eat lunch, I know. But this is aqua-tainment! I'm proud to say I've coined the phrase. Your guests can choose to participate or simply enjoy your pools. But in most facilities, guests spend more time on deck than in the water. Season-pass holders tend to spend the entire day at our facilities. For some, it can become boring. People have short attention spans today and crave entertainment. If the entertainment is good, they will return! It's a win-win situation that only requires creativity and energy. Here are some ideas for attracting different demographics and people with varying interests to your aquatic center.

Don't Preach to the Choir

In parks and recreation, professionals tend to sell to their current membership. In other words, we preach to the choir. We keep selling to our current customers and work less on finding new ones. Sure, it's important to keep your current members happy, give them a good value, and treat them well. But participation at aquatic centers and water parks is cyclical. Kids do grow out of our program, and often when the kids outgrow the facility, we lose the parents as well. Aqua-tainment is the answer to maintaining members, attracting new members, and targeting new, underserved populations.

Attract the Outdoor Crowd

Most facilities can accommodate paddleboards, kayaks, scuba diving, and snorkeling. Deck activities such as tai chi, yoga, bridge, and mah-jongg are sure ways to attract new members. Break the reputation of water parks and pools being just for kids by adding programs that adults enjoy. Facilities that have money to spend can invest in equipment that can become promotions, such as log rollers, aqua climbers, and inflatables. Whether these attractions are offered before or after public swim hours, adventure seekers will see your facility in a whole new light.

Dive Right In

Aquatic centers and water parks have long held dive-in movies where participants watch movies while floating in the water or lounging poolside. That big screen not only entertains but can also become a venue for paid advertising. You can sell time on the inflatable billboard as a movie preview or sell your own programs on the big screen.

Courtesy of David Guida.

Play isn't only for kids!

Appeal to Music Lovers

Looking to attract new members or those who haven't visited your facility for years? Appeal to them with free music performances. Look at your statistics and offer a free concert on your slowest evening. Open your gate and advertise the concert with a free one-hour swim. Pump up the event by calling it Sunday Night Coffee House. Offer music and flavored coffee for adults. The idea is to get them back into the facility and then impress them. You may get the active adults who haven't visited your site since the kids were young. Set up a table with information about your programs for active adults, and you have a successful recruitment event!

Who Let the Dogs Out?

Once a year, why not let your facility go to the dogs? Americans are crazy about their dogs. A Doggy Dip event lends itself to lots of corporate possibilities, great exposure among dog lovers, and the possibility of helping a local animal shelter. The photos and videos are hysterical, and the number of views is amazing. Again, it may appeal to a totally new group of prospective customers who also happen to love their dogs. You've earned their affection and in turn their loyalty.

Art at a Water Park

Do you have an art museum in your region? Partner with them to create an annual experience that your members will not forget and that can produce new members. At the Summit Family Aquatic Center in Summit, New Jersey, the Visual Arts Center judges an annual art contest on a hill at this beautiful facility. The center distributes foam-board sharks to families, who take them home to decorate in hopes of winning a family pass for the next year. The top three winners are exhibited at the Visual Arts Center, while the others are strung on fishing line throughout the facility's foyer. A sea full of sharks swims above the guests' heads for the rest of the summer. It might seem unusual for an aquatic center to partner with the art community, but it has been very popular. Both organizations benefit from the exposure, and the community gets overrun with sharks!

Do Something for Someone Else

Another type of special event can quickly become a promotional tool if you help someone else. Taking on a local fund-raiser for a charity is a great way to fill your park and gives you an opportunity to get key community influencers to talk about your facility. I'm not suggesting that you raise funds only for business, but often more visits and revenue do follow. Charitable commerce is prevalent in our society today. For example, shoe stores advertise that with every purchase of shoes, another pair is donated. You could donate a portion of every day pass during a certain time period to the charity of choice. Active volunteers will do the planning and sell tickets outside your entry area. Everyone wins, and you've given back to the community that hosts your aquatic center.

Watch for national trends in fund-raising and promotion. The summer of the Ice Bucket Challenge had us all dumping ice water on our heads to raise money for the ALS Association. From using large buckets in our family leisure pools to dumping water on our mascots, we were all cold and wet. The bounce from this type of charitable effort cannot be overlooked as a marketing tool.

As with everything you do at your aquatic center, you still have to focus on safety. Your aqua-tainment offerings cannot be so loud and distracting that a lifeguard's whistle can't be heard. You have to also exercise good judgment and not overstimulate your guests. They do need quiet time poolside, so balance is the key. If you are lucky enough to be planning for improvements to your facility or designing a new area, keep the idea of a performance area in mind. It will pay off over the years.

Marketing Tool Kits With Budgets in Mind

Traditional Tool Kit

- Press releases
- Seasonal printed brochures
- Fliers
- Posters
- Display ads
- Cable bulletin board announcements
- Announcement boards
- Website
- Word of mouth
- Repeat events

Starter Kit

- Mission statement
- Marketing plan
- Emergency media plan
- Directory of accepted news and media outlets
- Business cards, stationery, and support materials
- Web page
- Online photo and video library
- Social media outlets
- Agency brochure and promotional materials
- Seasonal brochures and promotional materials
- Agency color palette
- Agency logo
- Rate cards and rack cards
- Online user surveys
- Items from the traditional tool kit

(continued)

Marketing Tool Kits With Budgets in Mind
(continued)

Advanced Tool Kit

- Social media contests and sales promotions
- Sign plan
- Corporate sponsorship and advertising plan
- Press packets
- USP (unique selling proposition or tagline)
- Video presentations and closed-circuit TV programming
- Commercials and PSAs
- Billboards
- Electronic message board
- Recorded announcements on public address and music systems
- Personal histories and endorsements
- Staff photos and bios
- Name tags
- Stickers and stamps
- Step-and-repeat banners with logos
- Coupons and membership premiums
- Membership incentives
- Recorded telephone messages
- User surveys (online and on the property)
- Items from the starter tool kit

Sponsor-Driven Events

Corporate sponsorships and special events are nothing new in the waterpark business. But, partnering these two concepts is a real winner when you use the right approach. (Chapter 11 discusses the recruitment of corporate sponsors in more detail.) As corporations tighten their marketing budgets, the possibility of product placement and promotion is more likely now than ever. Aquatic venues have been successful in creating events that bring out the right demographics for your sponsors. Father's Day, Grandparent's Day, and other special family events can be sponsored and promoted entirely by your corporate sponsors.

Remember to let them do the work for you. Events such as Family Day can feature products and services in your community or on a national level. Allow sponsors to exhibit their products, distribute samples, and provide goods and services during community festivals at your aquatic center. For example, families could receive a photo of themselves in your lazy river, compliments of a local photography studio. The possibilities are endless. All of your corporate participants get to advertise their involvement. They each can display their signage and give out coupons at no cost to you. Soliciting companies that produce sunscreen, lip balm, shampoo, and baby products can often result in free samples to give out at your facility. It doesn't hurt to ask.

Don't even start to recruit corporate partners for events like this until you have a good handle on your demographics. Companies will need to know many people their product will be exposed to. They'll want to know income range, ages, and other details to determine if it works for them. They really want to know how many people they will reach and what the attendees' purchasing power is.

You might be thinking that an aquatic center or water park is an unusual location for this type of activity, but I beg to differ. You have parking, restrooms, sound systems, and all the amenities you need for hosting a major special event in and out of season—and attendees can swim too? Fabulous.

Tom Sawyer School of Marketing

At this point in the book, you're probably saying to yourself, this woman is nuts! Who has the time for all this work while running an aquatic operation? There are creative approaches to getting these promotions at your facility, with a little help from your friends. After all, Tom Sawyer did it.

When faced with the tedious job of whitewashing a picket fence, young Tom Sawyer made the task seem so fun that all of his friends begged to have a chance to do it. At the end of the day, the fence was painted, his friends were happy, and Tom never even broke a sweat. This classic tale is a perfect illustration of how you can maximize your revenue picture without adding to your personnel or operational expenses. I've coined this approach the Tom Sawyer School of Marketing. It's a way to get someone else to do the work, pay for your event, and thank you for the experience. Here are a few approaches to consider.

Sell Those Tickets! Fill Those Pools!

If you are searching for novel ways to add to your annual revenue and attendance, the Tom Sawyer approach may be right for you. Most aquatic facilities enjoy healthy attendance during peak hours but often struggle with attracting the midweek and evening crowds. In some cases it's hard to even justify staffing costs to stay open during slow times. With today's aquatic center designs, it's much more difficult to open and staff every amenity, yet guests expect every attraction to be open. This is not a burden; it is an opportunity.

Community organizations from the Boy Scouts to local first-aid squads are constantly searching for fund-raising events that can help to fill their treasury and serve as a social event as well. Your family aquatic center, recreation center, pool, water park, or any other recreation area just might be a unique fund-raising venue not often considered. This approach goes further than the traditional group sales event or buyout. Your group sales and marketing staff rarely need to even be involved. Don't have a group sales department or marketing staff? Then this chapter is right for you!

First, you need to identify the days of the week and times of day when your facility sees a dip in attendance. These are most likely Tuesday through Thursday and most weekdays after four. But this can change geographically, so be sure to do a thorough review of your attendance figures over an entire season to avoid overselling busier times. Remember, your goal is to fill your facility when it isn't otherwise busy.

For many aquatic centers, the entire month of July doesn't need any special promotions. However, June and late August are prime times for these types of events. The concepts can be as simple as declaring a Girl Scout Day at your facility. Visitors who wear part of their Girl Scout uniform that day will receive a discount on admission. All of the promotion is the responsibility of the organization. From fliers to social media and posters, the targeting organization will promote the event within the organization much more effectively than you or your staff will ever be able to do.

In many instances, such as in civic organizations, their communication network is strong and efficient. The organization will often also provide the entertainment in your facility for that day. For example, perhaps they will run a demonstration or the opportunity to earn a Girl Scout badge with an activity such as an AED demonstration, life-vest drills, or even kayaking or paddleboarding. What may be an activity for their group will certainly be entertaining for others to watch. They can showcase their skills and win the hearts of the public. They can also distribute materials about their organization to those in the aquatic center who may develop an interest because of the event.

In exchange for all their promotional efforts, the organization will receive a discounted admission price for members of the organization and their friends and family. They will also receive one to two dollars per person for their own treasury in return for their efforts. That type of fund-raising sure beats a bake sale!

This approach is a win-win proposition. Both your facility and the organization receive exposure in the community. You are viewed as a great community collaborator or corporate citizen. I like to call these types of promotions *reverse promotions* because all the work is up to others and you receive a benefit.

In most cases, the aquatic center is still open, it's still available to the general public, and guests get to learn about a great community organization. It's a fun way for a nonprofit to earn money and have a large-scale social event as well. You get to fill your park on a day that's usually slow. By the way, along with the Girl Scouts come grandma and grandpa, siblings, and friends. This may be the only exposure they have to your facility. Ultimately, it can also translate into new members.

Free Entertainment and a Recruitment Tool Too?

Another Tom Sawyer approach can help you to address all of those requests from dance troupes and karate dojos to perform at your aquatic center. Instead of settling for a rental from these types of community businesses, turn them into marketing opportunities for your facility. Scheduling performances of such groups as entertainment at your facility serves several purposes. Along with the performers come moms, dads, grandparents, and siblings who need to purchase a ticket to attend their performance.

Keep good old Tom Sawyer in mind as you plan these entertainment opportunities. Let the karate school do all the promotion and sales. In exchange, the participants get a free admission, while the spectators get a slight discount or a one- to two-dollar fee per ticket given to their treasury or charity of choice. Take a serious look at past attendance patterns and let your imagination go wild. Music schools, dance studios, cheerleading camps, and gymnastics studios are all anxious for performance venues that are affordable. Another idea is to hold a firefighters appreciation night. Firefighters get free admission with a discount for their friends and family who come along. Let them plan all of the special events and watch the fun begin. The possibilities are limitless, especially by using return coupons and other promotions that can be tracked. I guarantee that these efforts will result in return visits or season-pass sales from segments of the community that may never have entered your facility before.

Early Risers Love Long Courses

Masters swimmers, triathletes, and early risers love long-course swimming. Renting pools to area swim leagues and swim schools is common in many communities. Usually the only time pools are available is in the early morning. These rentals can be lucrative, but how can you balance the need for increasing your bottom line while your own members are begging for early-morning swimming? Why not combine the two needs and make it happen the Tom Sawyer way?

Require the team that is renting your morning time to allow one or two lanes for your fitness enthusiasts. Also require them to provide the lifeguards and supervisory staff in addition to their rental fee. You can then accommodate your early-morning swimmers' desire for long course, while it will not cost you a dime. In fact, you will make money while shifting the responsibility. The only requirement should be that the lifeguards have all the same qualifications that you require, and be sure to get a certificate of insurance. Not comfortable with other lifeguards outside your training? Go ahead and have them hire one of your own lifeguards. It still provides a service to your membership, sweetens your bottom line, and doesn't show up in your expense line items. A side benefit is your facility will be more attractive to fitness swimmers and athletes who must join to take advantage of the long-course training in the early morning. Without this training luxury, they might not consider your facility at all.

Scholarship Aid Made Affordable

One of the biggest challenges for any community-based aquatic center is making the facility affordable for families who can't afford the price of admission. The Tom Sawyer approach works just fine in this regard. Communities across the country have developed all sorts of responses to this need, most of which don't require a large expense to the aquatic center.

Banks, realtors, and civic associations can purchase tickets that are imprinted with their logo and are then distributed throughout the community by school nurses, social workers, and service organizations such as Boys & Girls Clubs. The companies and organizations that get involved receive recognition by the city council or your organization with a plaque for their headquarters. This enables children to enjoy the aquatic center with a sense of dignity and pride. The sponsoring organizations and corporations have the satisfaction of helping those in need while receiving the appropriate recognition.

I've come across a variety of truly creative approaches to providing scholarship assistance with dignity. Here are a few of my favorite approaches to reach those most in need of assistance. In Lafayette, Indiana, teens who volunteer in the parks get rewarded with rec dollars that can be used for admission to Tropicanoe Cove. Why not have big-barrel banks to fill with loose change near your concession stand? Get a local bank or business to match the annual yield from the barrel. This can be a great grassroots effort to help kids in the community.

Charleston County Park and Recreation Commission had one of my favorite scholarship campaigns of all time. They found the most novel combination of a public–private partnership with a dash of community philanthropy. With the help of Greenbax Enterprises and participating Piggly Wiggly supermarkets, any child in Charleston County could swim in one of the three water parks. With each visit to a Piggly Wiggly, you would receive Greenbax stamps in the amount of the purchase. Save up enough stamps and paste them in a book, and you could use them for a swim! Community organizations collected the books of stamps from folks who were not interested in redeeming them and gave them to deserving kids in the community. This was a winner for all the parties involved. The Charleston County aquatic facilities were beautifully illustrated in the Greenbax catalog, Piggly Wiggly got increased traffic at the checkouts and paid for each redeemed Greenbax booklet, and kids got to swim. Because everyone was welcome to collect stamps, no one needed to know if children saved their own stamps or if the stamps were given to them. Tom Sawyer would have loved living in Charleston County.

Memberships in aquatic centers are constantly adjusting as the demographics of the region change. Your promotions and special events need to be tailored to fill the gaps in membership and be as fluid as possible to remain successful.

Lessons Learned

- Entertainment doesn't have to be expensive.
- Entertainers are looking for audiences. You have the audience; they have the talent.
- Know your demographics and understand what companies need to know to support your efforts.
- Host special events on slower days to fill your aquatic center.
- Look at events as promotional tools, and use them to attract new prospective customers.
- Team up with organizations and local businesses, and they will help promote the event.
- Charitable events can help the community and improve your image as a good neighbor.

11

ENHANCE THE BOTTOM LINE WITH CORPORATE SPONSORS

Courtesy of David Guida.

Throughout this book, you've found references to corporate sponsorships and corporate partners. You may still wonder how corporate partnerships, sponsors, and collaborations relate to marketing your aquatic center. First and foremost, the more revenue you have from these types of partnerships, the more you will have to spend on improving your facilities. With increased revenue, you have a chance at increasing your budget, in particular what you can spend on marketing and promotions. Second, as stated in earlier chapters, developing these types of partnerships will increase your visibility. It creates a natural partnering in the areas of print ads, social media, television, radio, and promotions. You will now be able to piggyback on the marketing plans of your corporate partners.

Over the last couple of decades, corporate sponsorships at water parks and large aquatic facilities mostly centered on food and beverage service. At one time, getting a soda sponsor to give you a high-dollar sponsorship was much easier than it is now. These types of sponsorships are still out there but are now primarily based on sales. Cups, umbrellas, menu boards, and other items may still be provided to you at no cost, but a high sponsorship payment for a soda exclusive is reserved for those who are selling huge quantities of product. The entire industry has had to get creative, so you will have to be creative, too.

Finding the right balance of corporate sponsorships for your facility will be something of an experiment at first. Establish a balance between the number of corporate sponsorships you accept and the signage that usually comes along with deal. People are barraged with ads, product placements, and logos in every medium. The last thing you want is to take on so many corporate sponsors that your facility becomes overloaded with signage. The best advice I can give to aquatic centers who are starting to develop a corporate sponsorship campaign is to wade in carefully before you dive in too deep!

Excitement without a huge expense.

When to Start

If you are planning for a new facility, you are extremely fortunate in many ways. In this case, start creating your corporate sponsorship plans while the facility is being designed. Explore possible locations for sign placement. You will be able to get better prices on installing items such as shade structures if you install them during the initial construction of the facility rather than after the project is completed. Those savings can be passed on to your inaugural sponsors. After all, they are taking a chance on you without the benefit of actual attendance numbers and without truly knowing the demographics of those who will visit your facility in great numbers. Offering a preconstruction and postconstruction fee schedule for corporate sponsorship is brilliant and can be well received. If you prepare for corporate sponsorships during the construction phase, you will have more than adequate lead time for logo placement and signage. As each new corporate sponsor buys into your campaign, it gives you an opportunity for press coverage and creates a sense of excitement about the new facility.

Not building a new facility or adding a new attraction? No worries. Corporate sponsorship campaigns can be used by existing facilities and become an integral part of a capital improvement program for your aquatic center.

How to Start

Municipal aquatic facilities that want to embark on a corporate sponsorship campaign should first research the public contract laws in their state. Work alongside your administration and legal department, and a legal team if available.

At this stage, you should create a wish list. Inventory your aquatic center and identify amenities that have sponsorship potential. Don't think about capital improvements alone; consider equipment, supplies, goods, and services along with possible special events and programs.

Establish Sponsorship Levels

Almost every aquatic center that I have ever coached with regard to corporate sponsorship campaigns asks this question first: How do you establish the sponsorship levels? My best advice is use the actual cost of the items you want sponsors to pay for, plus an extra percentage to cover overhead costs. Include the expenses of signage, advertising fees, setup art charges, and any custom requests. Depending on the regional business climate, these overhead costs could be as high as twice the cost of the item. You might consider offering a discount for early buy-in. If so, take that into account when covering the cost of each item you want to purchase.

Get familiar with what local and regional advertisers charge for promotional time and coverage, and be competitive with the cost of these other options. Be careful offering exclusives to corporate partners unless the payout is large and long term. Try to have a variety of items to sponsor at a wide range of price points so that even the local mom-and-pop shops can participate.

Do Your Research

Collect rate sheets from local advertisers and explore the cost of television, radio, print media, tourism guides, regional magazines, community calendars, coupons, and Facebook and other web-based advertising. Study the companies who use these outlets. Schedule a time to talk with them to share how a sponsorship with your facility could benefit them. If they value other avenues of promoting their business, they will certainly want to hear what you have to offer.

Get your nose out of industry journals and be a student of magazines such as *Adweek*, websites like Pinterest, and web-based retailers. If you aren't a natural salesperson, find someone who is, or else acquire a taste for the art of the sale. Read books on sales and the advertising industry.

Sponsorship Types

- Direct advertising for an annual fee, such as posting a sign on your property or distributing coupons or products throughout the year
- Sponsorship of amenities on your property such as shade structures, slides, or life vests
- Sponsorship of special events with an opportunity for free tickets or priority seating
- Goods or services exchanged for sponsorship (trades)
- Premiums such as food, beverages, and samples
- Membership incentives that increase the perceived value of your membership card, such as discounts on products and services offered by the sponsor that members can take advantage of by showing their facility membership card

There is so much information now available online that you can certainly learn a lot through study and practice.

Create Sponsorship Policies

Establish how you will disseminate information about your sponsorship campaign. Write a mission statement, and have it formally adopted by your board or leadership. Make sure all of you are on the same page. You should also decide which staff members will be authorized to negotiate contracts. Designate one person who finalizes each sponsorship deal in order to ensure a sense of fairness and to protect the value of your sponsorship items.

As you write your corporate sponsorship policy, be sure to define each term used in the policy. Many of these terms may be new to you and your staff. Determine the length of the contract for each category of memberships. Describe how you will recognize your sponsors. Establish sponsorship levels based on cost and length of the contract. Define the entitlements and any special conditions that come along with each sponsorship level.

My biggest faux pas in selling corporate sponsorships was to allow a real estate company to sponsor a shade area and use its own corporate sign. Because the signage was emblazoned with "For Sale," it looked as

Support Materials

- Approach letters
- Sales-pitch script
- Invoices
- Terms and conditions documentation
- Contracts or agreements
- Indemnification forms
- Corporate opportunities packet (both hard copy and electronic versions)
- Press kit with articles and highlights about the aquatic center
- Promotional video, virtual tour, and display boards with site plans and visuals
- Testimonials from other sponsors, support documents, letters, and press
- Corporate honor roll sign at the facility entrance
- Sample newsletters and Facebook posts

if our shade structure were for sale! The colors on the sign didn't match our color palette, either. From that day on, I learned a valuable lesson: Establish sign and logo restrictions regarding size, color, and font. Don't compromise your facility for a sponsorship.

Approach Letter

The best corporate sponsorship deals are usually the result of in-person conversations. Even so, you need an approach letter to open the door or to leave behind with each potential sponsor. Create a printed sponsorship welcome packet, or create a website with a link to a pdf version. Make it as easy as possible for potential sponsors. In your approach letter, include the following:

- Attendance figures for your facility
- Demographics and buying power of your members and guests
- Benefits of sponsorships, such as incentives and privileges
- Sense of urgency, such as mentioning if a limited number of packages are available
- Invitation for conversation about creative alternatives; for example, sponsors may not have money to give you, but they may have product, and their ideas may be better than yours, so make it clear you are open to mutually beneficial solutions

Sell the Sponsorship

Most of us in the aquatic industry are not salespeople. Or are we? Do you always talk about your facility? Do you sell your programs and services? Do you speak to the press about your exceptional programs and special events? If so, then you are a salesperson. A corporate sponsorship is just a slightly different product. You must remember that you are selling advertising opportunities and corporate sponsorships, not begging for help. You aren't selling a name on the back of a baseball jersey; you are providing an exceptional opportunity to businesses that gives them exposure to your guests.

Become intimate with the benefits you can offer, and always be ready to sell. Only use quality printed and electronic materials, and make it as easy as possible for potential sponsors to access that information. Provide a tour of your facility, even if it is under construction. We are in a visually exciting business, and that can entice sponsors to want to be involved. Be sure to always keep your promises, and follow up with correspondence after a conversation. Be available and flexible. Stop talking and start listening to sponsors; ideas will sprout if you allow them to.

Find Sponsors

Identify businesses that currently advertise in some way in your community or market, and be ready to compare what you have to offer in terms of both cost and impact. Find a sponsor in one category, and then target others in that group. Become a member of the chamber of commerce, Elks, Lions, and other local organizations. Plenty of business is done within those groups. Make presentations to local organizations whenever possible.

Hospitals, realtors, pediatricians, chiropractors, and banks can be reliable targets, especially for safety items such as life vests, first-aid rooms, and lazy-river tubes. My favorite sponsorship of all time was a 20-foot (6 m) umbrella sold to a local newspaper. The umbrella read, “We’ve Got You Covered!” Explore nonprofit partners too; they have a story to tell and often have advertising budgets.

Remember to be a good partner with each of your sponsors. Don’t just take money from them; honor them and cherish the relationship. Bring your talents and resources to the table. Define how you can help your corporate sponsors increase their business within the partnership.

Courtesy of Gretchen Masterfano.

Splash and Learn while poolside adds entertainment value and shows your concern for your guests.

Plan for Success

Here I go again, giving you work assignments when you are already overworked. There are ways to secure corporate sponsors without burning the midnight oil. Recreation, marketing, and communication interns can be wonderful assets in developing these resources under your guidance. Some of my clients have hired salespeople on a percentage basis, while others have worked through an advertising agency. If you are a seasonal facility, the off-season is the time to make these sales calls. Often the end of the year is a great time to sell these types of partnerships, because some firms must spend down their budgets by year-end. Using a team approach is the best way for a busy aquatic manager. Educate your staff about your corporate sponsorship campaign, and they can talk it up when they hear someone is interested.

Aquatic centers of every size can reap the benefits of an aggressive corporate sponsorship program. Although the work necessary to establish a program may seem daunting, I've provided the basics you need to get started at any level. Once you score your first few corporate sponsors, you'll catch the fever. A boss of mine once said, "You would sell advertising on the back of your bathing suit if you could." I replied, "As long as I can get billboard rates, I'm available!" I have, however, sold the arms of T-shirts and the backs of jackets on numerous occasions. Have a plan, identify the tasks, make the assignments, and you are on your way.

Keeping Sponsors for the Long Term

- Foster the relationship all year long with notes, cards, and facility updates.
- Put sponsors on the list to receive your electronic newsletter, and highlight their contributions. Treat them like members.
- Provide a certificate of appreciation and a photograph taken on-site that your partners can proudly display.
- Tube and raft sponsors love having a tube for their own pool or for display at their office.
- Create a page on your website to include sponsor logos and links to their websites.
- Share the news and accomplishments of your corporate sponsors with your membership through newsletters and on-site signage.
- Admit any missteps as soon as possible, and make up for them.
- Always keep your promises.
- Treat your sponsors with the respect they deserve.

Courtesy of David Guida.

Happy sponsors, happy bottom line!

Lessons Learned

- Know your corporate sponsorship campaign well so you can sell at any opportunity.
- Never give away your power; always control the signage within your facility.
- In sales, listening is important. Listen more and talk less, and the ideas will flow.
- Consider trades for goods or services. Need a paint job? A painter may have paint and labor but not cash.
- Partners can come from nonprofit organizations, too.
- Real estate agencies, banks, chiropractors, children's clothing stores, and hospitals have been successful targets for me in the past. Think of sponsors who want to get their product or service in front of families and children.

REFERENCES

American Marketing Association. n.d. "Dictionary." www.ama.org/resources/Pages/Dictionary.aspx?dLetter=B&dLetter=B.

Brennan, B. 2009. *Why She Buys: The New Strategy for Reaching the World's Most Powerful Customers.* NewYork: Crown Publishing.

Burns, D. 2011. "Who Are the Baby Boomers?" *Baby Boomer Magazine*. April 2011. http://babyboomer-magazine.com. (article on site discontinued)

Disney. 2007. "Disney Catering to the Wine Connoisseur." October 29, 2007. www.diningindisney.com/disney-catering-to-the-wine-connoisseur.

Hendrie, J. R. 2004. "Destination Marketing 101: Take Care of Mom." www.htrends.com. (article on site discontinued).

Lindstrom, M. and P. Seybold. 2004. *Brand Child*. Philadelphia, PA: Kogan Page Publishing.

Lipton, L. 2013. "Visiting Walt Disney World Without Kids." *Conde Nast Traveler.* May 14, 2013. www.cntraveler.com/stories/2013-05-14/how-to-visit-disney-world-without-kids-lauren-lipton.

McLuhan, M. (1964) 1994. *Understanding Media: The Extensions of Man*. Cambridge, MA: MIT Press.

McNeal, J.U. 1999. *The Kid's Market: Myths & Realities*. Ithaca, NY: Paramount Publishing.

Merriam-Webster, s.v. "brand (n.)." Accessed May 21, 2018. https://www.merriam-webster.com/dictionary/brand.

Merriam-Webster, s.v. "brand (v.). "Accessed May 21, 2018. https://www.merriam-webster.com/dictionary/brand.

Merriam-Webster, s.v. "mascot (n.)." Accessed May 23, 2018. https://www.merriam-webster.com/dictionary/mascot.

Popcorn, F., and L. Marigold. 2000. *Eveolution*. New York: Hachette Books.

Price, R. 2016. "The Medium Is the Message: How New Media Affects the Gospel." Last updated May 12, 2016. www.sagu.edu/thoughthub/the-medium-is-the-message-how-new-media-affects-the-gospel-2.

Townsend, D. 2008. "'Signs' of Safety. Accessed May 23, 2018. ISHN . https://www.ishn.com/articles/87227-signs-of-safety.

Work, S. "How Loading Time Affects Your Bottom Line." *KISSmetrics Blog*. Accessed May 23, 2018. https://blog.kissmetrics.com/loading-time/.

ABOUT THE AUTHOR

Judith Leblein Josephs has more than 40 years of experience working in a variety of roles related to aquatic facility management. She is a featured speaker at state, national, and international aquatics conferences and training seminars and has a knack for making learning a memorable and enjoyable event.

After 20 years in the public sector, Josephs was with Water Technology Inc. for 12 years as their marketing and operations consultant. She has served as an operations coach for dozens of facilities of all sizes, both municipal and privately owned properties, and in 2006, she formed her own consulting business, Judith Leblein Josephs Enterprises LLC. She has clients across the country, including the City of Providence, Rhode Island, and all of the aquatic venues for the Salvation Army Eastern Territory.

Josephs knew that she would someday return to the public sector, and in 2007 she was recruited by the City of Summit, New Jersey, to serve as their director of community programs. She had a role on the design team that renovated the community pool, now known as the Summit Family Aquatic Center. Recognized with *Aquatics International*'s 2014 Best of Marketing Award, the Summit Family Aquatic Center's mascot, Shark Diddy, graced the cover of the magazine.

Josephs' specialty in marketing, promotions, and television and radio production has proven quite valuable to all of her employers and clients. She has an unprecedented 12-time record of winning the Speaker of the Year distinction from the World Waterpark Association (WWA), and she was inducted into the WWA Hall of Fame in 2003. In addition to numerous WWA Splash Marketing Awards and Industry Innovation Awards, she received the WWA Board of Director's Award in 2011.

She has also helped launch hundreds of new aquatic venues as the instructor of WWA's *Ready, Set, Go! A Guide to Getting Started* program. Her how-to lists and articles published in major industry publications are used by aquatic operators worldwide.